S0-BJA-612

SIX

TRANSLATED BY

DONALD RICHIE

AND MIYOKO

WATANABE

KABUKI PLAYS

THE HOKUSEIDO PRESS
TOKYO 1963

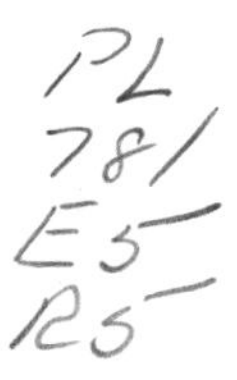

FIRST PRINTING, 1963

Published by the Hokuseido Press
3-chome, Nishikicho, Kanda, Tokyo

Published by The Hokuseido Press
3-12, Kanda-Nishikicho, Chiyoda-ku, Tokyo

CONTENTS

INTRODUCTION

These six plays, and *Kanjincho*, are the repertoire of the Kabuki's 1960 American tour, and these translations were made for that occasion. Since they were intended to be heard rather than read, being broadcast by Miss Watanabe and Mr. Richie during actual performance, each member of the audience hearing through closed-circuit, ear-phone transistor radios, the spoken English had to synchronize precisely with the spoken Japanese.

The method of translation was consequently somewhat different than is usual. Miss Watanabe made literal translations of all the plays and Mr. Richie experimented with the English until it fit the play not only literally but also stylistically, the ideal being a translation so unobtrusive that it would soon cease to be "heard," just as dialogue-titles for foreign films soon cease to be "seen."

In America, the plays were cut, just as they are often cut in Japan. *Chushingura* is represented by four of its best scenes; *Kagotsurube* is given without some of its middle acts and without its usual ending; and some of the choral passages are missing from *Musume Dojoji*. These cuts are retained in these translations and, in addition,

INTRODUCTION

THE STAGE DIRECTIONS—OCCASIONALLY DIFFERENT FROM THOSE TRADITIONAL AT THE KABUKI-ZA—ARE THOSE USED IN NEW YORK AND WEST COAST PERFORMANCES.

THE TRANSLATORS ARE GRATEFUL FOR THE HELP AND ENCOURAGEMENT THEY RECEIVED, IN PARTICULAR FROM LINCOLN KIRSTEIN, DR. SHIGETOSHI KAWATAKE, DONALD KEENE, MISS AYAKO SOMA, FAUBION BOWERS, ERIC KLESTADT, AND ICHIRO SAWADA.

TOKYO, 1963

KAGOTSURUBE

THE COURTESAN

A KABUKI DRAMA WRITTEN BY KAWATAKE SHINICHI III AND FIRST PERFORMED IN 1889.

THE FIRST SCENE IS IN NAKANO-CHO, THE LIVELIEST SECTION OF EDO'S FAMED LICENSED QUARTER, THE YOSHIWARA. JIROZAEMON, A WEALTHY MAN FROM THE COUNTRY, AND HIS SERVANT, JIROKU, ARE SEEING THE SIGHTS. JUST THEN THE FAMOUS COURTESAN, YATSUHASHI, PASSES WITH ALL OF HER ATTENDANTS. THOUGH HE IS A SIMPLE COUNTRYMAN AND, FURTHER, IS DISFIGURED BY SMALLPOX SCARS, JIROZAEMON FALLS IN LOVE WITH HER AT FIRST SIGHT. SHE, SEEING THIS, LAUGHS AND PASSES ON.

THE SECOND OF THESE SCENES FROM THE PLAY TAKES PLACE IN A ROOM AT THE TACHIBANAYA TEAHOUSE WHERE JIROZAEMON AND YATSUHASHI HAVE BEEN IN THE HABIT OF MEETING NOW THAT HE HAS BECOME A REGULAR CLIENT. HE APPEARS, BRINGING WITH HIM TWO MERCHANT FRIENDS. THEY APPRECIATIVELY REMARK UPON THE MUTUAL AFFECTION THE TWO SEEM TO FEEL FOR EACH OTHER.

THE THIRD SCENE IS IN ANOTHER ROOM WHERE EINOJO, YATSUHASHI'S LOVER, IS ANGRY BECAUSE HE HAS HEARD THAT JIROZAEMON INTENDS TO RANSOM THE COURTESAN, FREE HER OF HER DEBTS,

AND SET HER UP AS HIS OWN MISTRESS. GOMPACHI, YATSUHASHI'S 'OWNER' AND TO WHOM HER DEBTS ARE OWED, APPEARS, AND THE TWO MEN EVENTUALLY PERSUADE THE COURTESAN TO LEAVE OFF SEEING JIROZAEMON.

THE FOURTH SCENE IS IN A LARGE BANQUETING ROOM AT THE TACHIBANAYA. A PARTY IS IN PROGRESS IN CELEBRATION OF JIROZAEMON'S FREEING YATSUHASHI. WHEN SHE APPEARS, HOWEVER, SHE IS COLD, SAYS THAT SHE REFUSES TO SEE JIROZAEMON AGAIN AND WILL GIVE NO REASON FOR HER BEHAVIOUR. WHEN JIROZAEMON DISCOVERS THAT SHE HAS A LOVER HE SAYS HE WILL GIVE HER UP AND RETURN TO THE COUNTRY. YATSUHASHI, WHO DOES NOT REALLY DISLIKE JIROZAEMON, KEEPS UP HER PRETENSE AND THE PARTY BREAKS UP WITH JIROZAEMON LEAVING EDO.

THE FIFTH SCENE OCCURS FOUR MONTHS LATER, IN AN UPPER ROOM OF THE TEAHOUSE. JIROZAEMON HAS RETURNED AND YATSUHASHI APPEARS, CONTRITE. EVERYONE THINKS HE HAS COME TO RESTORE RELATIONS. THEY LEAVE THE COUPLE ALONE. HE POURS SAKE FOR HER THEN TELLS HER TO DRINK FOR THIS WILL BE HER LAST. DRAWING HIS SWORD, HE KILLS BOTH HER AND A SERVANT GIRL WHO HAS COME BRINGING A LAMP. IN LATER SCENES HE MAKES HIS ESCAPE, ONLY TO BE LATER CAPTURED.

CAST

YATSUHASHI, *A Grand Courtesan*
SANO JIROZAEMON, *A Wealthy Man from the Country*
GENAN JIROKU, *His Servant*
SHIGEYAMA EINOJO, *Yatsuhashi's Lover*
TSURIGANE GOMPACHI, *Yatsuhashi's 'Owner'*
TAMBEI, JOSUKE, *Friends of Jirozaemon*
OKITSU, *Mistress of the Teahouse*
KOKONOE, YAEZAKI, AYAME, KAKI-TSUBATA, *Courtesans*
OTATSU, *A Courtesans' Attendant*
OITO, OKOTO, *Geisha*
YOSUKE, *A Servant*
OSAKI, *A Maid*
HANCHU, CHOJI, *Entertainers*
SERVANTS, TEA-SERVERS, ETC.

SCENE I

A running curtain; the Nakano-cho district of the Yoshiwara. Jirozaemon and his servant, Jiroku, appear.

JIROKU: I have heard great tales of Edo's Yoshiwara, but I did not believe that it was so splendid a place.

Yet, we should be returning.

JIRO: Yes, so we should. Yet will not the guardian at the Great Gate charge a fee? A toll for our having come inside to look about?

JIROKU: It is indeed so splendid that possibly they would not show it free of charge. I shall certainly not feel myself again until we are outside the Great Gate.

JIRO: Well, then Jiroku; let us just be careful; come along.

From stage left comes the oiran-dochu, *the procession of the courtesans. Jiro sees the celebrated Yatsuhashi; she sees him staring and laughs at him; he continues staring; he has fallen in love. After the procession has passed:*

JIROKU: Come, master. Let us go. Come, come. Let us return.

JIRO: Ah . . . to return . . . I no longer want to.

SCENE II

Okitsu, the mistress, is with Gompachi, the owner of the courtesan, Yatsuhashi.

GOMPACHI: Then you mean to say that no matter how I beg you will not give me the money?

OKITSU: Naturally I shall not give it to you. Go home, wash your face, return and ask in half a year.

GOMPACHI: Well, I cannot stay here forever; I will wash my face, as you say, and come back. But I will also teach you not to make a fool of me. I will pay you back for this.

After he has gone, Yosuke scatters salt to purify the air.

Jiro, with his friends, Josuke and Tambei enter from the hanamichi; *the mistress welcomes them.*

KITSU: You are all most welcome; please come in.

We have all been talking about you; the courtesan Yatsuhashi will be here shortly.

JIRO: I have two guests with me today and since we stopped to see the sights at Okuyama, it became later than we had thought.

YOSUKE: Do you wish to go to Yatsuhashi, or shall I send for her?

KITSU: Please call her.

YOSUKE: Very well, mistress, I shall go. Oh, the courtesan Yatsuhashi is coming now.

KITSU: She must have been most impatient, to have come so soon.

TAMBEI AND JOSUKE: Ah, this gentleman is a lady's-man indeed.

JIRO: Ah, it feels quite wonderful to be here.

Yatsuhashi enters with her attendants.

KITSU: Well, courtesan, please come over here and sit down.

Then, if you will pardon me, you are all most welcome.

TAMBEI: This is the first time that I have had the honor of setting eyes upon the renowned Yatsuhashi, and I am quite overcome.

JOSUKE: The real this is ever so much better than are those printed pictures sold of her everywhere in the country.

JIRO: Look at her.

And how do you like that?

Now all of you will understand why I feel as I do.

KITSU: From now onwards you two gentlemen must visit us just as frequently as he does.

TAMBEI: Ah, to be sure, to be sure. Just seeing the lady makes me envious.

JOSUKE: Here, here. You must not praise her so much. If you do, Jiro will become jealous.

JIRO: Why not at all. She is, after all, for sale. The days I am not using her, pray buy her yourselves.

YATSU: Oh, what hateful things you do say. If a guest appears whom I do not like, then I myself do not appear.

She playfully touches his hand with her long-stemmed pipe. It startles him.

TAMBEI: Certainly, tonight at Hyogoya here . . .

JOSUKE: . . . We have no objections to being entertained.

JIRO: Gentlemen, you must understand my feelings in the matter.

TAMBEI: Of course, of course. If we were to be extended such courtesies . . .

JOSUKE: . . . and were to be treated so royally, it would be almost more than we could bear.

TAMBEI: Seeing all this, one cannot believe one's own eyes.

JOSUKE: One thinks one is dreaming.

JIRO: To not believe one's eyes would seem to prove that

. . . they know nothing of the licensed quarter.

SCENE III

Another room in the teahouse

YATSU: Tonight there are many guests and no more rooms are free. Please be contented with this.

She begins to arrange cushions for him.

EINOJO: This is not necessary. I merely wanted to see you and hear from you your intentions.

YATSU: What is the matter, there is nothing wrong in accepting a mere cushion.

EINOJO: There is no need for one as I shall not be staying. Your cruelty is like an illness and if I stayed I might contact your heartlessness.

YATSU: What do you mean? That you will not be staying. Why?

EINOJO: Look into yourself and you will know the reason why.

YATSU: What do you mean? I should know?

EINOJO: Listen, Yatsuhashi, I know that you have decided to be ransomed off and to throw me over.

YATSU: What? Where did you hear that?

EINOJO: Where I heard it is none of your affair. It is enough that, since you are utterly faithless, I have come to complain.

YATSU: Part of what you have heard is not untrue, but how could I be so faithless to you, and is it not unkind to have believed that I was capable of such faithlessness?

GOMPACHI: Oh, so far as that goes, I am witness that you are utterly faithless.

YATSU: Then, it was you who told him . . .

GOMPACHI: Since you have no parents I stand in your parents stead. If you were bought out by a wealthy country gentleman, I too should profit from the transaction. Yet, would not your actions be inexcusable to Einojo, with whom you have exchanged vows to all eternity? What would you do and how would you explain this to Einojo?

YATSU: The fact that I did not tell of this ransoming is the best proof you could have. Please rest assured of my intentions.

EINOJO: Then, if you are so clear in your own mind, you will have opportunity to demonstrate your decision. Jirozaemon is giving a party here tonight. At that time, if you formally refuse, we will gladly clear you of all suspicion.

YATSU: Then I should throw over a guest who has treated me so well?

GOMPACHI: What do you say? It will be difficult for you to do, and the teahouse will be most disturbed.

EINOJO: If you will not end all relations with him, then give me back my pledge and thus end all relations with me. From tonight we will be complete strangers.

YATSU: But how could I do that?

EINOJO: You will break his vows or mine.

YATSU: If that be so . .

GOMPACHI: Then you throw over Einojo?

YATSU: Well, I . . .

TOGETHER: Come, come, come.

EINOJO: Give me your answer . . . I am waiting.

SCENE IV

A large banqueting room at the Tachibanaya where Jirozaemon has gatherea together a number oj guests. A party is in progress.

OSAKI: Yatsuhashi has arrived.

Yatsuhashi appears.

YATSU: Jirozaemon, do pray forgive my having kept you.

BANSHIN: The guests at the Nagatoya would not would not allow her to depart. Finally, she had to make them leave her go.

YATSU: This evening I am disturbed. Please do not speak to me.

JIRO: If our mistress is not feeling well, Otatsu, we had best call a physician.

OTATSU: Yes, yes.

YATSU: There is no need to call a physician. Only one thing disturbs me.

JIRO: If something disturbs you, then it is bad for you. What would it be? Please tell me quickly.

YATSU: May I really tell you?

JIRO: Of course. Do tell me. What is the matter?

YATSU: It is that whenever I meet you, whenever I speak with you, I become more and more disturbed.

JIRO: That may well be so when you are already disturbed. I will keep silent. And you others, please be quiet until she is herself once more.

YATSU: No, no. That is not what I mean.

JIRO: What do you mean to say by that?

YATSU: That I cannot stand the sight of you, sir.

JIRO: What?

Gompachi and Einojo appear, eavesdropping. Yatsuhashi turns and begins a celebrated scene, one of the genre called aisozukashi, *a cutting-off-of relations scene. She does not actually dislike Jiro, but it must appear that she does.*

YATSU: For some time I have been contemplating refusal; I have been tempted not to come to this party, making apologies as best I might to host and guests. Yet, since you, our host, are here a guest where I have always been well treated and made welcome, I put off this resolution day by day. I put it off so far as to hear your intention to buy me out, making me your own. But this, sir, from that first talk onward has been to me distasteful to an extreme. And it is now that I take the opportunity to decline and to respectfully request that you see me no more.

JIRO: It would seem, dear lady, that I have offended. Please forgive me for this. And if you do not want to return with me to Sano, then I will undertake to purchase for you a house in Edo and will see that you are comfortable in it. But tonight we shall not talk of this. Please calm yourself, leave us now and rest.

YATSU: Sir, I rest when I will. I have good reason . . . No, there are no reasons. Only that I dislike you and decline your buying me.

KITSU: Courtesan, I do not know of this indisposition, but I do know that you are putting me in a most difficult position. As for your being bought out, it was I who made all arrangements and, as you must know, it was tonight that this was to have been officially announced to our assembled guests. You must reconsider, you must not speak so strongly.

KOKONOE: Until now you have not expressed such dislike. Why then do you turn so suddenly against your patron. If you have a reason then why did you not make me your confidante and tell me all?

YATSU: There is no reason. It is enough that the thought of being ransomed, bought by him, makes me ill. Please leave me alone.

NANAKOSHI: You mean to say that there is no other, deeper reason?

YATSU: In the life of our profession nothing is more distasteful than coddling the unwelcome guest. You, Kokonoe, should understand my feelings in this.

TAMBEI: Well, well, Master Jirozaemon, and what it you were telling us but the other day? You would have us come to Edo. You would have us visit Yoshiwara. You would there show us your prodigy of popularity. Sir, you have boasted. And I, having seen and heard, would venture to say that you have boasted, sir, merely upon how completely you can be scorned.

JOSUKE: That someone as beautiful as the famous Yatsuhashi, should care for someone like you, I frankly doubted, but you insisted. Now that I have seen this, however, I find myself to have been wholly and completely in the right.

JUROKU: Yes, just look. Back at home I told my master that it was the business of prostitutes to lie and cheat their customers, that you would indeed be made a fool of if you thought they really loved. And now . . . See? . . . you are paying for it.

OTATSU: Courtesan, what is the matter? . . . to treat a guest in this way; a guest moreover so valuable a customer.

HANCHU: We two were always invited to the master's rooms . . .

CHOSHI: And, though it may be rude to say, we found him most well-behaved . . . for a country gentleman.

OITO: And faithful too, for there is no rumor telling of visits to another. Why then do you behave in this manner?

OKOTO: When ladies and their patrons fall out, we are all made uncomfortable.

BANSHIN: Even we who work here in the Yoshiwara do not understand this strange outburst and do not know what she is doing. Yet, if something troubles you, then speak openly and honestly tell us all.

OTATSU: Please smile again and tell us everything is all right.

ALL: Yes, please do so.

YATSU: I, perhaps, do not count for much, yet, still, I am Yatsuhashi who rules over these three inner blocks of Nakano-cho, and if I once say no, you might ask a million times and I would still refuse.

KITSU: Then such a favorable proposal as this . . .

BANSHIN: . . . you mean to say you would decline?

ALL: Is this then true?

YATSU: Money means nothing to me. I will do what I want.

OTATSU: Then, right in front of him . . .

ALL: . . . you reject the ransom?

YATSU: Yes, once and for all, I decline.

JIROKU: Yatsuhashi, consider what you are saying. Since my master first laid eyes on you he has come to see you upon every visit to Edo. This has continued until now your ransoming has been arranged. Now, suddenly, you tonight refuse. This may indeed be the custom of the licensed quarters but it is too much. I have been silent but now I would speak. If you would decline, why then decline, but, doing so, return to him the money he has spent on you.

YATSU: It is not I who once asked him to come to me. Rather, it was he who involved himself more and more. And however much more you speak, from loyalty to your master, such illogic as yours means nothing to me.

JIROKU: This, madame, is logical. You have led him, you have chained him. You have cheated him. If logic shall not aid my revenge, then force will. I am Jiroku from Nanao in Noto and I have lifted hundred-weights in stone; in strength I am equal to all. If you do not yourself return these sums then I shall see to it that in some form returned they be.

JIRO: Here, here, why so excited? The more we show our anger the greater the shame. Please sit down and be quiet.

JIROKU: It makes me angry.

JIRO: I have told you to be quiet. Go.

JIROKU: Yes.

JIRO: Say no more, be quiet.

JIROKU: Yes.

Then Jiro, mastering his own anger, fighting his own bitterness, begins his most famous scene, a passage noted for the beauty of its diction, the restraint of its feeling.

JIRO: Courtsan, you are too unkind!
Nightly you pleasure yourself with different men,
A veritable river down which you float, rising and falling.
Your heart is for the guest of today
While the guest of yesterday goes forgotten.
And I, last night, could not sleep for the thought of today,
The thought that upon this very night you should have been mine.
Waking, I awaited the autumn night's dawning,
Envisioning this evening and all it would bring.
Yet now I discover that I am thrown over
And thrown though I am, I cannot now begin to blame you.
Rather, though but a country man, I would ask you
Why, oh, why did you not tell me so from the beginning?

I am known here within Yoshiwara;
I have come here for your sake alone,
But I have grown famous for coming
And a courtesan's praise is well-known.
The hosts and the guests all know me,
And now must I disappear?
Humiliated, must I vanish from here?
It would be but decent, think, courtesan,
To consider my honour, as a man.

YATSU: Yes, famous you are, for you come here nightly.
Yet, if you had not come so frequently how much less would be your shame now. I am sorry for you and can understand your feelings, yet from this you will have learned a valuable lesson and will come here no more.

JIRO: Then you hate me as much as this?

YATSU: But consider and you will understand that I am being very kind in telling you this before undergoing the ceremony planned for my being brought out in such a public manner, a ceremony which has been the talk of Yoshiwara these many days.

Jirozaemon sees Einojo.

JIRO: Ah . . . then one of those two men whom we saw before, loitering in the corridor, one of them is your lover?

OTATSU: No, no, master—they were the guests from Yotsuya.

YATSU: To hide my doings is not my habit. As you have guessed, sir, the man is a masterless samurai by the name of Einojo Shigeyama and he is indeed my lover.

JIRO: Then, madame, you had your reasons. My thanks for your having finally told me. Not another word shall I say and I have dropped all thought of ransoming you.

YATSU: If you have understood, then there is no reason further why we should stay here, then I am relieved. Let us go to another room.

KOKONOE: Wait, Yatsuhashi, you have completely thrown him over, despite what we have said?

YATSU: I am completely tired of him.

KOKONOE: And so you would soil what honour we have in our life?

YATSU: Yes, Kokonoe, please forgive me.

After Yatsu has closed the door she assumes a famous tableau wherein she express her feelings. She does not hate Jiro, yet—an actress—she half believes her own role. Now, outside, she betrays her true feelings.

TAMBEI: You, sir, have talked much of your province of Sano but let me tell you, sir, that this banquet-scene which we have witnessed will shame into the very earth all the worthy folk of Sano. Let us, gentlemen, begin again at another place; let us liven our spirits, sirs, and attempt to wipe out the shame.

JOSUKE: Come, all of you, to the next party.

HANCHU: Thank you kindly, sirs, but the gentleman has engaged us.

JIRO: Please go with them; do not hesitate because of me.

HANCHU, OITO AND OKOTO: If that is so . . . then begging your pardon, we shall go.

JIROKU: Here, all of you, are you going to leave my master alone?

TAMBEI: It is none of your business . . .

BOTH: . . . Shut up.

JIROKU: Now I am furious. A terrible thing has happened and one not to be put up with.

KITSU: I am really most sorry. But wait, I shall go to Yatsuhashi's teahouse and shall return only after having arranged everything to your satisfaction.

JIRO: No, please do not go. Having heard of this Einojo, her betrothed, I know that she will never love me. I have, you see, given up all thought of her. I will return home, coming again later.

KITSU: And you have given up all hope?

JIRO: To be so thrown over, yet to happily return home;
Indeed, one knows not what kind of fool to call me.

KOKONOE: Oh, Jirozaemon, please come if only once again.

JIRO: Yes, I might just return to . . .

KOKONOE: What?

JIRO: I said, I must return home . . . and now I must go.
Madame, you have been kind to me. Thank you very much.

SCENE V

An upstairs room at the Tachibanaya, four months later. Jirozaemon comes up, followed by the others.

OSAKI: Welcome, Jirozaemon. Please come this way.

KITSU: We had thought of coming to visit you in the country, but after what happened . . . we contented ourselves with speaking of you frequently.

JIRO: Here is the rest of the bill for the last time, and something extra as well. Please take it.

KITSU: Well, if you say so, I will take it. Thank the gentleman.

ALL: Thank you very much.

YARITE: Be careful going up the stairs, Yatsuhashi.

OTATSU: Jirozaemon, Yatsuhashi said she felt so ashamed that she could not show her face to you, but I have at last persuaded her to come.

JIRO: Bring her here quickly.

YATSU: I really should not show myself to you but Otatsu said that you had been so good as to call for me, and that it would have been even more rude had I not come. I hope you will forgive my coming.

JIRO: If you speak in this fashion then I in turn feel ashamed. At that time it was September and all flowering affairs come to a sudden end. Now, from today, let us have a new beginning, and you are to treat me as a new guest.

YATSU: So then today we have a first meeting, and a new guest . . .

JIRO: . . . with Yatsuhashi, the most famous courtesan of them all.

KITSU: And from now on, through frequent meetings you will progress through the necessary stages until finally you reach the state you were before and a happy time that will be.

HANCHU: And with that . . .

ALL: We all feel much relieved.

JIRO: I did not think I would meet you all again but am overjoyed to discover that I have. But, at present, I have a secret matter to discuss with Yatsuhashi and after we have done there will be a splendid banquet, then I shall return home.

KITSU: I can well understand you two wanting a private talk.

BANSHIN AND YAEZAKI: We will show our delicacy, giving them needed privacy, and all leave.

OTATSU: And, master, once you have finished . . .

ALL: . . . clap your hands.

JIRO: Come up in good time.

BANSHIN: Then we shall be waiting downstairs.

JIRO: Yatsu, go and look at the staircase, to see that they are all down.

When her back is turned he takes off his tabi *and puts them under the cushion, so that he will not slip when using the sword.*

YATSU: I will.

And now what do you have to say?

JIRO: To restore relations in this way is a very great pleasure to me.
As a sign that the pleasure is mutual, please take this cup.

YATSU: I was very worried but these are kind words, and I with pleasure gladly take this cup.

JIRO: And I shall pour for you.

YATSU: Oh, this is too great an honour. But you have filled it too full. Please, you drink half.

JIRO: Oh, no, since it is poured, you must drink it all.

YATSU: But it is too much.

JIRO: Drink it. It is a farewell cup.

YATSU: What do you mean? Farewell cup?

JIRO: Yatsuhashi! Sometime ago you dared to shame Jirozaemon!

She tries to rise but he steps on her kimono and prevents her doing so.

JIRO: I knew that prostitutes cheated their patrons; but I was infatuated: I would have made you my own but then, for the sake of Einojo, you cheated me at your own banquet; you shamed me in the very midst of my love.

YATSU: Then all you said now, of reconciliation, is not true?

JIRO: My hatred, my revenge, has been growing daily but I have hidden it away within me. Today I come for revenge.

YATSU: While I understand your anger, there are also reasons for my actions. Please listen to me.

JIRO: It is now too late for reasons; I will have your life. How you humiliated me!

He kills her. The servant appears with a lamp.

SERVANT: I have brought a lamp. Did you ask for a lamp? I am sorry, I did not think of it before. Well, here it is, if you care for anything else . . .

He kills her as well, then assumes a stance.

JIROZAEMON: Ah . . . sword . . . you cut . . . well!

CURTAIN

MUSUME DOJOJI

THE MAIDEN AT DOJO TEMPLE

ADAPTED FROM A NOH PLAY AND FIRST PERFORMED IN 1753.

THE SCENE REPRESENTS THE PRECINCTS OF THE DOJO TEMPLE, DOMINATED BY A GREAT HANGING BELL. PRIESTS ENTER, CELEBRATING THE DEDICATION OF THE NEW BELL. A BEAUTIFUL YOUNG GIRL APPEARS, SAYING THAT SHE HAS COME TO SEE THE DEDICATION. THE PRIESTS AT FIRST REFUSE HER ENTRANCE.

THEIR REASON IS THAT MANY YEARS AGO, A VILLAGE GIRL WAS IN LOVE WITH A DOJO PRIEST AND, WHEN HE SPURNED HER ADVANCES, TURNED HERSELF INTO A GREAT SERPENT. TERRIFIED, THE PRIEST HID UNDER A BIG BELL. THE SERPENT COILED ITSELF AROUND BOTH BELL AND PRIEST AND MELTED THEM.

THE PRIESTS FINALLY ALLOW THE GIRL IN AFTER SHE HAS SAID THAT SHE WILL DANCE. THIS SHE DOES—AND HER DANCE MIGHT BE INTERPRETED AS THE PHASES OF A WOMAN'S LIFE, FROM INFANCY TO MATURITY. AS SHE DANCES THE PRIESTS FEEL THAT THERE IS SOMETHING STRANGE ABOUT HER. SHE CHANGES COSTUMES DURING THE DANCE AND WITH EACH CHANGE THE PRIESTS GROW MORE FRIGHTENED. THEN THEY REMEMBER THAT THE

SERPENT TOO CHANGES HIS COSTUME, HE CASTS HIS SKIN. THE PRIESTS RISE TO DRIVE HER AWAY BUT SHE CLIMBS ONTO THE BELL AND THERE REVEALS HERSELF AS INDEED THE SERPENT-DEMON.

THE TEXTS OF NOH ARE OFTEN FRAGMENTARY IN THE SENSE THAT THEY ARE SOMETIMES COMPOSED OF, OR AT LEAST INCLUDE, POETRY FROM VARIOUS SOURCES, APHORISMS FROM EARLIER PERIODS, AND SONGS IN THE STYLE POPULAR AT THEIR FIRST PRESENTATION. THE AUSTERITY OF THE NOH ITSELF OFTEN COMPRESSES THESE VARIOUS ELEMENTS INTO A STYLISTIC WHOLE. WHEN THE NOH DRAMA IS ADAPTED BY THE KABUKI, HOWEVER, IT OFTEN HAPPENS THAT THIS STYLE IS SACRIFIED IN FAVOR OF ONE OF PARTS MAKING UP THE THEATRICAL WHOLE. IN *MUSUME DOJOJI*, FOR EXAMPLE, THE TEXT ITSELF IS TREATED AS A MERE PRETEXT FOR THE DANCE, AND THIS PARTICULAR KABUKI IS THOUGHT OF AS A DANCE-PLAY, RATHER THAN AS A DRAMA. IT IS REGARDED AS SOMETHING ANALAGOUS TO THE CONCERT-ARIA. THUS THE WORDS OF THE CHORUS MEAN VERY LITTLE INDEED—IN FACT, THAT THE MAIDEN IS ACTUALLY A SERPENT-DEMON IS NOT EVEN MENTIONED IN THE TEXT, AND NEITHER IS HER FORMER ADVENTURE AT THE DOJO TEMPLE, INFORMATION NECESSARY IF ONE IS TO FOLLOW THE PLAY AS DRAMA, BUT QUITE BESIDE THE POINT IF ONE THINKS OF IT AS PURE DANCE.

THEREFORE THE ENGLISH RENDITION IS SOMETHING EVEN LESS THAN APPROXIMATE. RATHER, IT IS AN EXTREMELY FREE ADAPATION IN WHICH A KIND OF SENSE HAS BEEN IMPOSED UPON THE TEXT ITSELF. THERE ARE AT LEAST SEVERAL INTERPRETATIONS DIFFERENT FROM THE ONE BELOW, BUT THIS ONE, MEANT TO BE HEARD RATHER THAN READ, AT LEAST INDICATES THE ATMOSPHERE OF THE ORIGINAL.

CAST

THE MAIDEN
PRIESTS
CHANTERS AND MUSICIANS

The scene is the Dojo Temple.

The priests appear on the hanamichi.

PRIESTS: Have you heard, have you heard?
Today is the ceremony for the dedication of the bell.

CHORUS: Soon the moon will wane and the tide will come in . . .

And now, with fluttering dress, a maiden comes:
Though I am shy, I have come to pray to the god of marriage.
If you think that this is foolish of me, laugh if you will.
The night that I sleep with my lord . . .
The morning after a lovers' meeting . . .

The more I think of it . . .
How disagreeable.
The morning bell . . .
And one would want to break the striking hammer . . .
. . . my heart hurries as I too hurry along the sand banks,
Arriving at the Dojo Temple.

The maiden appears.

FIRST PRIEST: It seems that a woman has come.

Let us question her.

Who are you?

MAIDEN: I am a dancer who lives nearby.

FIRST PRIEST: And what business have you here . . .

PRIESTS: . . . at this temple.

MAIDEN: I have heard that there will be a ceremony for the bell.
I have come a long way to respectfully attend.

FIRST PRIEST: We shall allow you to do so. Please enter.

And here is a golden helmet with which you will please dance for us.

MAIDEN: I shall.

She takes the golden helmet and retires.

2ND PRIEST: While she is preparing herself . . .

3RD PRIEST: . . . then . . .

4TH PRIEST: . . . let us dance our prayers.

The priests dance.

1ST PRIEST: It seems that she is ready. Let us watch her.

The maiden, wearing the golden helmet, begins a slow dance in the Noh style.

CHORUS: Beside the cherry-blossoms, there are pines.
Beside the cherry-blossoms, there are pines,
And the evening bell is resounding.
I hate the sound of that bell.
When it sounds, it speaks of the mutability of all earthly things;
And when the midnight bell rings it is heard while we hover between life and death;
But the morning bell speaks of the encompassing compassion of Buddha.
These bells speak truly to all who listen . . .
And the clouds of the future are cleared away.
The eternal truth, like a clear moon, gives light to all.

She removes the helmet and both music and dance grow faster as the chorus begins a song in the popular style.

I cannot disclose my love, and my hair is disheveled,
My heart is disheveled.

And a pitiful thing is the changeable heart of man . . .
. . . for man is evil.
I am used to the freer ways of the city . . .
. . . but yet I am a lotus . . .

The sense of the passage depends upon an untranslatable pun, a play upon the word hasu—*the word for lotus and also a word used to indicate looseness in a woman. This pun is visually indicated when the maiden changes her kimono from red to blue.*

The chorus is repeated and the maiden dances in the many-tiered 'lotus' head-dress.

Clusters of plum blossoms, clusters of cherry-blossoms,

And one does not know which is older brother, which is younger brother.

Yet they are all beautiful.

She retires and the priests dance.

The iris and the camillia,

We do not know which is elder, which younger sister.

Yet they are all beautiful.

Two priests dance together.

CHORUS: From west, from east, from south,
All come to see the blossoms . . .

. . . how beautiful,
This blossoming maiden.

The maiden returns in a lavender kimono and dances with a tenugui, *a short length of cloth sometimes used as a towel.*

The love I learned without learning . . .
And why do I paint my lips and blacken my teeth?
It is because I love you, because
I am happy.

In the end we shall be reunited.
And until then I shall say nothing
For even written vows are false.
Are you lying, are you telling the truth?
I could not bear to wait, so
I have come to see.

I restrain myself,
Hoping never to become jealous,
But I am, after all, a woman.
And do not understand the heart of a man.
I do not understand
The heart of a man.
For it is evil.
It is evil.

With hatred she looks at the bell,
And as cherry-blossoms carry dew within their hearts,
So does her heart carry tears.

The sense of this passage, in both words and dance, is that she is indeed the vengeful spirit of the snake, returned. She almost allows this to be seen by the priests, then remembers and the cherry-blossom simile is rendered harmless with:

But now the cherry-blossoms are falling,
Falling to the ground.

During this passage she retires then comes on again in a yellow kimono bearing a drum design, and carrying with her a small hand drum with which she dances, later exchanging it for a pair of hand cymbals.

For this latter dance, the chorus sings again a passage in the fashion of a popular song:

CHORUS: The month of May, the month of May.
The maiden, rice-planting,
Sings a song of planting the rice.
She has wet the hem of her dress and the bottom of her sleeve.
The pretty flower maiden . . .
. . . with disheveled hair, with disheveled heart.

As she dances she approaches the great hanging bell which descends until it rests upon the stage. She quickly mounts it.

And the more I think of it . . .
The more that I think of it . . .
The more unendurable it becomes.

She stands atop the bell.

She put her hands around the bell.

She strikes a pose.

She leaps . . .

And carrying the bell with her
She disappears.

CURTAIN

TSUBOSAKA REIGENKI

THE MIRACLE AT TSUBOSAKA TEMPLE

ADAPTED FROM A BUNRAKU PLAY BY TOYOZAWA CHIKA AND FIRST PERFORMED IN 1887.

IN THE FIRST SCENE SAWAICHI, A BLIND MAN, AND HIS WIFE ARE TALKING IN THEIR HOUSE. HE SUSPECTS HER OF INFIDELITY BUT SHE TELLS HIM THAT SHE HAS BEEN MEETING NO LOVER, RATHER, SHE HAS NIGHTLY GONE TO PRAY TO KANNON, GODDESS OF MERCY, FOR HIS RECOVERY. SHE URGES HIM TO LIKEWISE PRAY AND THEY GO OFF TO THE TEMPLE.

THE SECOND SCENE IS BEFORE THE HALL OF KANNON AT THE TSUBOSAKA TEMPLE. THE MAN AND WIFE ENTER AND AFTER SHE HAS TOLD HIM TO BEWARE OF THE DANGEROUS RAVINE NEAR THE TEMPLE, SHE LEAVES HIM TO PRAY. AFTER SHE HAS GONE, HE GROPES HIS WAY TO THE CHASM, AND, FEELING THAT HE NO LONGER WISHES TO LIVE, THROWS HIMSELF INTO IT. SHE RETURNS, SEARCHES FOR HIM, AND EVENTUALLY SEES HIS BODY FAR BELOW. DESPAIRING, SHE LEAPS AFTER HIM.

THE THIRD SCENE IS THE RAVINE BELOW THE TEMPLE WHERE LIE THE BODIES OF MAN AND WIFE. THE GODDESS KANNON APPEARS AND MERCIFULLY RESTORES THEM TO LIFE AFTER WHICH

THE JOYOUS COUPLE FIND THAT SAWAICHI HAS HAD HIS SIGHT RESTORED AS WELL. JOYFULLY, THE TWO ADDRESS A PRAYER OF THANKS TO THE GODDESS WHILE THE CHORUS CLOSES THE PLAY WITH A PAEON TO THE MERCIFUL KANNON.

CAST

SAWAICHI, *A Blind Man*
OSATO, *His Wife*
THE GODDESS KANNON
CHANTERS AND MUSICIANS

The house of Sawaichi, the blind man; the shoji *opens and Sawaichi appears, playing the* samisen *and singing:*

SAWAICHI: 'Even the call of the birds and the sound of the bells sink into my ears. And the more I recall, the more the tears flow . . .

At the end of the song, Osato, his wife, appears.

OSATO: You took the samisen out today. You must be in good spirits.

SAWAICHI: Do I appear to be in good spirits, playing my samisen?

OSATO: Yes.

SAWAICHI: Actually, I am not. I am deeply depressed. In fact, I am so depressed that I feel like dying and ending everything.

I would like to ask you something. Come here and sit down.

It is not really important, however. I have always meant to ask you and until now have had no opportunity, but this seems the right moment.

It has been three years now that we have been living together and we should know each other's hearts. Why do you hide it from me, why not tell me straight out?

OSATO: What do you mean? During these three years that I have been your wife I have hidden nothing from you, nothing even the size of a drop of dew. But if there is something which disatisfies you, then tell me frankly, for such is the manner of man and wife.

SAWAICHI: Then I will tell you.

OSATO: Please do so.

SAWAICHI: Then, I will tell you. Listen well, Osato. Since we have become man and wife there has not been a morning that you have been in your bed after four. I am blind and it would not be surprising that you should not care for me. So, if you have found another man, please tell me so. I have often heard from others that you are very beautiful, yet I am not jealous. I am resigned to my fate. Do tell me.

The gidayu-chanter begins his commentary accompanied by samisen.

CHORUS: Although he controls himself and does not shed a blind man's tears, yet his heart is lonely. And, as she hears this, Osato is surprised and she clings to him.

OSATO: However poor we may be, do you think that I am a woman who could leave you for another man? It is unreasonable and it is untrue. Ever since death took my parents I have lived with my uncle and have been brought up with you. I have lived with you as though with an elder brother, a brother older by three years.

CHORUS: You are unfortunate, pock-marked . . .

OSATO: . . . and moreover blind.

CHORUS: Yet, though we have lived in poverty, we are still together. We are man and wife whether at the bottom of the sea or in the midst of fire, and we will remain so throughout eternity.

OSATO: And in order to heal your eyes . . .

CHORUS: I rise daily when I hear the four o'clock bell and go to Tsubosaka, to the Hall of the Goddess Kannon, climbing the mountain roads. This I have been doing for these three years. Every day I have been praying for the return of your sight, waiting daily for an answer to my prayers. But the Goddess Kannon seems not to hear me and now I have begun to hate her.

OSATO: And now, not knowing what is in my heart, you say that I have been seeing another man . . .

CHORUS: . . . and this makes me angry.

The tears of the faithful wife are sincere and Sawaichi, hearing for the first time of these things is much affected and his words of apology are tear-choked.

SAWAICHI: Osato, I have no words with which to apologize to you. Forgive me, forgive me. I did not know. I am nothing but a complaining blind man. Dear wife . . .

CHORUS: . . . forgive me.

He folds his hands and apologizes. His sleeves are wet with tears.

OSATO: You need not apologize to your wife. Your suspicions are now laid away, and I would be content to die even now.

SAWAICHI: Your saying this makes me deeply ashamed of myself. Yet, even having such faith in Kannon as you do, look at these eyes, they are no better.

OSATO: Your body and my body are as one. Rather than making these complaints, let us go now to Kannon. Calm your heart and together we will pray, together.

SAWAICHI: So great is your faith that if we pray to Kannon it may end as that saying which states that the Lord Buddha made flowers blossom even on withered trees. If this could be so, then take my hand and lead me.

OSATO: Yes.

CHORUS: Lead me by the hand, lead me by the hand, he says, and, hearing this, the pleased wife gets herself ready. With heavy hearts and deep vows they make off in the direction of the temple Tsubosaka.

OSATO: Here is the stream. Be careful.

SAWAICHI: There we are.

CHORUS: They both start on their way.

The scene changes to the temple before the Hall of Kannon. A temble bell rings and the sound of the drum simulates the sound of wind in the mountains.

CHORUS: Filled with rocks, filled with sand, the garden of Tsubosaka . . .

SAWAICHI: Osato, although I do not think our pleas will be heard, acting upon your advice, we have come this far. Still, I feel that nothing will happen and that my eyes will not heal.

OSATO: Again you say this. To be faithful means to be patient. You should calm your heart, pray with all your strength, and then everything will be granted by the merciful goddess. Instead of wasting our time on this kind of talk, let us go quickly to her and pray.

CHORUS: Encouraging him thus . . .

SAWAICHI: I shall go, then, as you say. From tonight on, I shall fast here for three days. Now you go home as quickly as possible and take care of things.

OSATO: I am pleased by what you say. I shall go home and then come back as soon as I can. You wait for me. But, Sawaichi, we are on a high mountain and on the right there is a deep ravine which you should go nowhere near.

SAWAICHI: There is a ravine on the right of the mountain? Well, from tonight on I shall be here anyway, having a tug-of-war with the goddess.

They both laugh at this attempted joke and the chorus continues:

CHORUS: Though worrying, the wife laughs, not knowing that this is to be the last time she sees her husband alive.

SAWAICHI: Listen, Osato. Take good care of yourself.

OSATO: What?

SAWAICHI: Be careful on your way home.

CHORUS: Osato quickly disappears and Sawaichi, remaining behind, alone, not being able to restrain himself any longer, collapses, weeping.

SAWAICHI: How unworthy I am of such a wife. She has looked after me all these years and has been so gentle with me. And I doubted her. Oh, forgive me, forgive me.

CHORUS: So saying, he abandons himself to grief.

SAWAICHI: I must not cry, I must not cry. I remember her saying that to the right of this mountain is a deep ravine . . . Fortunately, there is no one around to see. Yes, I will destroy myself.

CHORUS: He rises, calms his grief-torn heart, and gropes his way. The bell of dawn is sounding as he hurries to meet his last moment of life. Leaning upon his staff he finally reaches the rocks.

Sawaichi totters to the brinks, sticks his staff into the ground and executes a mie.

The terrible rushing of water in the valley far below sounds like a greeting from the other world, a welcoming from Buddha.

He places his stick upon the ground . . .

SAWAICHI: May Buddha's blessing be upon me.

CHORUS: And so saying, he leaps. Thus dies this pitiful man.

His wife, out of breath, hurries up the path, worried and anxious, and finally reaches the top.

OSATO: Sawaichi, Sawaichi.

CHORUS: Although she looks for him there is no voice, there is no one there to answer her searching.

OSATO: Sawaichi, where are you, Sawaichi?

CHORUS: She sees something by the light of the moon. She looks deep down into the valley and there, to her grief, she sees in the light of the shining moon the corpse of her husband.

OSATO: Oh, Sawaichi has . . .

CHORUS: Even if she wanted to fly into that valley, she has no wings. And though she screams and wails, her only answer is the echo from the stony valley walls.

OSATO: Sawaichi, Sawaichi, why did you do this, why did you fling yourself into this ravine? I have not minded the difficulties of these years. I have been patient. And every day I have prayed to Kannon for help. Oh, help us, help us. There has not been a day when I have not prayed, and now this has happened. Left alone, what shall I do, what shall I do? Oh, is there anyone more wretched than myself?

CHORUS: But I cannot foretell the future. I did not know that this would be the final parting from my husband, the man with whom I pledged vows to last through both the worlds. But perhaps this sad fate of mine is due to something in a previous existence . . .

OSATO: A punishment . . . ?

CHORUS: A sin . . . ?

Oh, how pitiful, how pitiful.

OSATO: The blind man, who cannot see this world . . .

CHORUS: On his journey to death travels from one darkness to another.

OSATO: And who will lead him? I am certain he will become lost.

CHORUS: Oh, my loved one, my beloved, she cries, and her tears swell the waters of Tsubosaka. Then, at last raising her tear-stained face . . .

OSATO: I shall waste no time on grief. All of this was pre-ordained in a previous existence. I am resigned to my fate. Let me embark with my husband upon this voyage of death.

CHORUS: Hurrying, leaning upon this staff he left behind, the staff he has bequeathed, chanting: 'Lead me ahead to God . . .'

OSATO: May Buddha's blessings be upon me.

CHORUS: She leaps into the valley and joins her husband.

Oh, what a pitiful end for such a faithful wife.

The scene changes. The valley bottom, the corpses of the couple. Kannon appears.

CHORUS: Ah, the majestic figure of the merciful goddess, Kannon.

KANNON: Hear me, Sawaichi, hear me. Because of the virtue and fidelity of your wife I have bestowed upon you both a longer life. Henceforth be devout, make a pilgrimage to the thirty-three shrines and thank the merciful Buddha. Hear me, Osato; hear me, Sawaichi.

CHORUS: And as the words of Kannon fade, so does her majestic figure. As the valley gradually lightens, both, not knowing what is real and what is dream, lift themselves up.

OSATO: Oh, it is you, Sawaichi. Oh, Sawaichi. And it seems to me that you can see.

SAWAICHI: What are you saying? How could my eyes be opened?

OSATO: But they are open.

SAWAICHI: Yes, it is so. My eyes have opened, they have opened.

But who then are you?

OSATO: I am your wife.

SAWAICHI: You are my wife? But you are too beautiful to be my wife. Wait, let me hear your voice. Osato?

OSATO: Yes.

SAWAICHI: Well, I am very pleased to meet you.

OSATO: What are you saying, silly.

They laugh at this joke, then Sawaichi says:

SAWAICHI: Then did you, out of fidelity, throw yourself into this ravine?

OSATO: Yes.

SAWAICHI: I am unworthy of it. And now my eyes have opened, thanks to Kannon's . . .

OSATO: . . . repeated miracles.

TOGETHER: Oh, thank you, thank you, Kannon. We are unworthy, we are most unworthy.

CHORUS: It is not to be wondered at that they are filled with joy.

OSATO: Let us right here and now give a prayer of thanks.

SAWAICHI: For the first time I see the light of the sun.

CHORUS: Has there been a miracle? Unseeing eyes have opened and it is as though he is newly-born. Oh, how joyous that they are together again, this couple, so devoted to one another that not even a drop of water could force its way between them. Today is indeed a joyful day. Sawaichi sees the morning sun, he no longer needs his staff, and in praying, he can see the morning sun. All praise to the ten thousand gods and to Buddha and to the goddess Kannon, through whose power the rocks of Tsubosaka will rise, its garden will fill with water, and even the sands of the garden will glisten like paradise. This is the marvelous proof of the mercy and might of the Goddess Kannon.

The curtain is drawn; the couple is on the hanamichi. *Through habit Sawaichi begins to feel the way with his staff. Osato smiles.*

OSATO: Here, Sawaichi. You can see now.

SAWAICHI: Oh, that is right, Osato. Well, let us go.

They exit down the hanamichi.

CURTAIN

MIGAWARI ZAZEN

THE SUBSTITUTE

ADAPTED FROM A KYOGEN BY OKAMURA SHIKO

THE SINGLE SCENE OF THE PLAY IS THE TRADITIONAL KABUKI VERSION OF THE NOH STAGE UPON WHICH THE INTERLUDES, THE KYOGEN, ARE TRADITIONALLY GIVEN. A YOUNG LORD, YAMAKAGE UKYO, IS BURDENED WITH A WIFE OF FORCEFUL CHARACTER NAMED TAMANOI, BUT BEFORE HIS MARRIAGE HE HAD A BEAUTIFUL MISTRESS NAMED HANAGO. THOUGH HIS WIFE KEEPS HIM FAIRLY WELL IN LINE HE ONE DAY RECEIVES A LETTER FROM HIS MISTRESS AND DECIDES TO VISIT HER AT ALL COSTS.

HE TELLS HIS WIFE THAT HE HAS DECIDED TO GO TO A NEARBY TEMPLE AND PRAY FOR SEVEN DAYS AND SEVEN NIGHTS, HIS WIFE IS SUSPICIOUS BUT LETS HIM GO, THOUGH ONLY FOR A DAY. HE, OVERJOYED, SENDS FOR HIS SERVANT, TARO. DISGUISING TARO IN HIS OWN COAT, YAMAKAGE TELLS HIM TO STAY THERE UNTIL HE RETURNS, THEN RUSHES OFF TO SEE HANAGO.

HIS WIFE APPEARS, OSTENSIBLY TO BRING FOOD, AND QUICKLY DISCOVERS THE PLOT. SHE TAKES THE COAT FROM THE SERVANT AND PUTTING IT ON DECIDES TO WAIT FOR THE RETURN OF THE ERRANT HUSBAND. SOON HE IS SEEN, QUITE

DRUNK AND ALL THE MORE RIDICULOUS IN THAT HE IS WEARING ONE OF HANAGO'S GARMENTS. THINKING THAT HE IS SPEAKING WITH HIS SERVANT HE DESCRIBES IN GREAT DETAIL EXACTLY HOW HE SPENT HIS TIME. THIS HE DOES IN A MIMED DANCE IN WHICH HE REPRESENTS BOTH HIMSELF AND THE LOVELY HANAGO. FINALLY, HE PLAYFULLY TAKES THE COAT FROM THE SUPPOSED SERVANT AND DISCOVERS TO HIS HORROR HOW HE WILL HAVE TO PAY FOR HIS NIGHT OUT.

CAST

YAMAKAGE UKYO, *A Lord*
TAROKAJA, *His Servant*
TAMANOI, *His Wife*
CHIEDA AND SAEDA, *Maids*

ACCOMPANYING CHANTERS AND MUSICIANS

The Lord Ukyo appears.

UKYO: I live in the suburbs and a year ago when I visited the western provinces I stayed at an inn called the Osa, it was in Nogami in the land of Mino, and there a lovely maiden named Hanago served me saké. Well, recently she has written me again and again saying that she longs to see me but, alas, the old shrew who is my wife will not let me leave her side for even a moment and so I cannot go to see Hanago and this worries me very much.

My, but I wish there were some way that I could see her.

He ponders.

Oh, I have a good idea. I will call the old hag out and put the idea into execution.

UKYO: Wife, wife, are you there?

CHORUS: She immediately appears.

Ukyo and Tamanoi would appear mutually attached yet now her husband's mind seems wandering, and there is something in him of the light and care-free air of spring.

She, sensing nothing, speaks.

TAMANOI: And you have called me for what reason?

UKYO: Please come over here.

TAMANOI: And what is it?

UKYO: Well, nothing more than this. Recently I have had a succession of bad dreams and so I want to make a pilgrimage.

This is what I wanted to tell you.

TAMANOI: And what must you do to make this pilgrimage and how long will it take?

UKYO: Well, I must visit the various temples throughout the country and so it may take a year, or perhaps even two.

TAMANOI: Oh, how sad, how sad.

Turning to her maids

Chieda and Saeda. Please stop our lord from leaving me.

She weeps; Ukyo turns to go; the two maids stop him.

MAIDS: As you say, madame.

CHORUS: And saying they will not let him pass, they stop him.

All three women join in a dance which quite effectively stops the baffled Ukyo.

UKYO: Now I realize that you are doing this because you care for me very deeply. And for this I am grateful. But, please, do let me get on with this pilgrimage.

CHIEDA: If your heart is set upon it, then perform it in such a way as would please your wife.

SAEDA: You may perform the pilgrimage here at home.

TAMANOI: You say that the pilgrimage can be done here at home?

CHIEDA: Yes, allow me to explain.

You will stop before the household Buddha and will chant *Great is Buddha* one million times; you will after that happily dance the necessary rite in the manner of the priest Kuya.

SAEDA: And, besides this, there are the winter austerities, and the purification by abolution, and the ascetic practice of silence.

CHIEDA: And there are such miraculous things as the...

Pantomime supplies the meaning.

Here at home perform the religious rites...

TOGETHER: ... we beg of you.

UKYO: But how impious that would be of me. How could I, a man of no importance, presume to practice such ascetic self-discipline here.

TAMANOI: But I will not allow you to leave the premises.

UKYO: Oh, dear...

CHORUS: My heart is far away, my dear, dear Hanago. Stopped by the thorns at home, my dream of rose-like bliss has come to nothing.

And so he turns his head this way and that, wondering what to do and thinking deeply.

UKYO: Oh, I have a good idea.

I will lock myself up for seven days and seven night, right here in our own chapel at home.

TAMANOI: Now, that is a much better idea. And I

will stay close by your side and see that you have quite enough hot water and tea.

UKYO: Oh, no. Women are considered evil.

If I were to look at a woman, I might as well not meditate at all.

You had best stay far away.

TAMANOI: Well, then, I will not permit this seven-day meditation.

UKYO: Then you would not allow me to realize this great aspiration of mine? Oh, please, I most humbly beg of you.

He literally begs and Chieda, feeling sorry says:

CHIEDA: Dear Madame, our lord is so eager that he even clasps his hands in prayer and begs us.

SAEDA: Yes, madame, you are perhaps a bit too strict, telling him he cannot do this and cannot do that.

CHIEDA: If he so wants to meditate . . .

SAEDA: . . . then please permit him . . .

TOGETHER: . . . to do so.

TAMANOI: Truly, it is as you say.

Then, I will give you my kind permission, but only for one night may you perform this thing you call meditation.

UKYO: You mean for one night alone?

TAMANOI: Two nights are absolutely forbidden.

UKYO: Well, then, it cannot be helped. So, I will perform my meditation for this single night.

TAMANOI: Then I will see you early tomorrow morning.

They bow and are about to leave when Ukyo calls:

UKYO: One more thing, wife. It is said that it is difficult to attain Nirvana if the meditation is disturbed. So be certain that you do not come to see me.

TAMANOI: I will not disturb you.

UKYO: Yes, please do not.

CHORUS: Her heart still concerned with her husband, the wife, accompanied by her maids, leaves.

After they are safely gone, Ukyo allows himself laughter.

UKYO: She is a clever one, but, after all, she is only a woman.

Ah, but I fooled her.

Well, first I must call Tarokaja for I have something to discuss with him.

UKYO: Here, here, Tarokaja, are you there?

TAROKAJA: Yes, sir.

The servant appears.

UKYO: Are you here?

TAROKAJA: Yes, my lord.

UKYO: You are very quick today.

TAROKAJA: I must say, you are in a good mood today.

UKYO: It is but natural that I am in a good mood. Today I have received permission to spend one night by myself, and I am going to visit my dear Hanago.

TAROKAJA: That is more wonderful than I had thought. But, what excuse did you give to so escape for this one night?

UKYO: She would not let me go without good reason. So I told her that tonight I would meditate in the chapel and thus got leave to stay all night.

TAROKAJA: That is still better.

UKYO: Concerning which I have a favor to ask you. Would you help me?

TAROKAJA: And what, may I ask, does this favor consist of?

UKYO: Well, it is this.

She faithfully promised that she would not come to visit me, but I know the old shrew. She will hide herself behind something or other and watch me all night long.

So, since it will only be for a single night, would you please substitute yourself for me?

TAROKAJA: I would like to obey you, but please excuse me from this particular duty.

UKYO: And why is that?

TAROKAJA: Well, let me explain.

I am afraid of your wife . . .

CHORUS: She loves you very dearly and when you are at home she is always pleasant and smiling; her cheeks as rosy as those of the Goddess Otafuku.

But, oh, when she discovers the trick, she will become fearsome and probably beat me to death.

Please, I beg you . . .

. . . do not ask me.

TAROKAJA: Please . . . please.

UKYO: What, are you afraid of that old witch and not of me?

Stand at attention!

I will kill you now!

TAROKAJA: Now, wait, please wait.

I will do whatever you command.

UKYO: Truly?

TAROKAJA: Yes.

UKYO: Surely?

TAROKAJA: Yes, very surely.

UKYO: Well, I was just joking with you.

TAROKAJA: Well, it is not a very nice joke.

UKYO: It is only because I am so eager to see Hanago.

Wait.

You sit down here.

He seats his servant on the lacquered box at one side.

TAROKAJA: I do not understand any of this.

UKYO: And then you wear this around your shoulders.

He covers his servant with the coverlet used for all-night meditation, then closely observes him from several angles.

Good, good. No matter which way you are looked at, you look absolutely authentic. Now, even if the old shrew should come, you must absolutely not take this coverlet off.

TAROKAJA: Naturally I will not take it off.

UKYO: And I will come back home soon. Now stay just that way.

Do not say a word.

TAROKAJA: Please come home as soon as you can.

UKYO: Then, I am on my way.

TAROKAJA: Wait, my lord. If you are going to see Hanago, it may seem impolite to ask you, but please give my very best regards to her maid—she is named Kobai.

UKYO: So that is it. And you were friends with this Kobai, were you not?

TAROKAJA: I know it is an imposition, but . . .

Distressed lest his message go astray, he stands up and begins walking over to his lord. Then both begin laughing.

UKYO: Here, here. Whoever heard of someone in meditation walking about?

Sit down and be quiet.

TAROKAJA: Yes.

UKYO: Say nothing at all.

TAROKAJA: As you say, sir.

BOTH: Farewell, then. Farewell.

CHORUS: Farewell . . . farewell . . . and evening draws near.

Unnoticed by anyone he is off to enjoy himself.

UKYO: Oh, happy, happy me. I am off to see my dear Hanago.

CHORUS: And so saying, off he goes.

Ukyo hurries down the hanamichi.

TAROKAJA: And, sir, please come back soon. Please come back before your wife finds everything out. And listen, my lord. When you see Hanago please do not forget to ask her to give Kobai my very kindest regards . . .

He begins to walk about.

TAROKAJA: Oh, dear. Whoever heard of anyone in meditation walking about.

But it is quite uncomfortable.

He sits down again and pulls the coverlet over him.

CHORUS: Left behind is the husbandless coverlet. Ah, this couple is deeply in love but he must meditate, and concentrate his spirit upon the Buddha.

Overcome by loneliness for her dear husband, the wife comes to spy upon him.

The wife appears.

TAMANOI: I permitted my husband to undergo the ascetic exercises of meditation for this one night, and I promised that I would not visit him, but I know he must be very uncomfortable, and so

I have decided to watch over him, but quietly and secretly, and from this shadowed place.

She hides and watches.

Now what sort of thing is this?
Oh, it appears to be very uncomfortable indeed.
And seeing him thus I simply cannot bear to stay away.
Oh, I will have the food sent for which I have prepared.

Here, Chieda, Saeda, are you there?

CHORUS: Answering her call, the maids, holding their hands befittingly and reverently, bring out the golden-coloured tea and the sweetly fragrant cakes.

Chieda brings out a tea cup and Saeda carries a dish of cakes. The wife faces Tarokaja.

TAMANOI: My dear husband, I know that I promised that I would come nowhere near you, but how could I stay away, seeing you in such an uncomfortable state. You know the saying that 'saké sweeps away sorrow like a broom,'? Well, later shall I bring you some saké?

TAROKAJA: Yes!

He has happily forgotten who he is supposed to be; now he remembers and begins shaking his head: no, no.

TAMANOI: But you will not accept even tea?

CHORUS: Oh, you are unreasonable, you are cruel. Even if you are meditating and communing with Buddha, it is not nice at all that you will neither speak to me nor let me see your face.

After all, it is a woman's privilege to complain.

And you do so irritate me!

So saying she draws closer.

TAMANOI: At least, husband, let me see your face.

Maids, remove the coverlet!

CHORUS: They place their hands upon and . . . suddenly pull it off.

The two are much surprised!

TAMANOI: What! It is Tarokaja!

You no-good, you! Now where did my husband go?

And you had better tell me!

TAROKAJA: Wait, wait. I will tell you. He went to visit his dear Hanago.

TAMANOI: Oh! Even you say *dear* Hanago. It is *bitch* you ought to say! Bitch!

TAROKAJA: Oh, yes, yes. I meant, Hanago the bitch.

And because he wanted to visit Hanago he asked me to cover up with this coverlet.

CHORUS: I told him, my lord, I do not want to, but he threatened to kill me and so I had no choice but to wear it.

TAROKAJA: Chieda and Saeda, please, you too help apologize for me.

CHORUS: Even Tarokaja, always happy, fears the thundering hag and cowers, feebly apologizing the while.

TAMANOI: What? Did he say he would kill you if you did not substitute for him?

TAROKAJA: It is precisely as I say.

TAMANOI: Well, since you have truthfully confessed, Tarokaja, I will forgive you for your part in this. But now you will please allow me to sit where you were sitting and to wear over me this robe of meditation.

TAROKAJA: Oh, my, you will be putting me in a most awkward position. Please, not this. I will do anything else but this.

TAMANOI: Oh, so you fear only my husband and not . . . myself?

Very well then, I shall punish you. Is that all right?

TAROKAJA: Wait, wait. Yes, you may wear the coverlet. I will do anything you say, so long as you spare my life.

TAMANOI: Well then, hurry and put it over me.

TAROKAJA: As you say, madame.

CHORUS: The maids likewise assist and drape her with the coverlet, after which they retire.

TAROKAJA: Well, you cannot tell the difference. You look as pretty as a flower.

CHIEDA: You are the perfect image of our lord.

TAMANOI: Then I look like my lord, do I?

Very well done; very well done!

Now you all go into the next room.

TAROKAJA: Thank you very much.

CHORUS: They all bow and quietly retire to the next room.

The three leave.

Then the bell of dawning sounds . . .

He did not sleep well last night; he is unkept; his hair is dishevelled, it hangs like the willow.

And about him floats the fragrance of interlocked sleeves, while the image of his beloved still hangs before his sight.

Ukyo appears, rather drunk, his hair undone; even more ridiculous in that he is wearing one of Hanago's robes.

CHORUS: She accompanied me for a long way, then bade me farewell.

I looked back and saw her still standing.

Oh, how we hated to part.

The saké we drank fired our blood and I sang the melody Ogikazashite . . .

CHORUS: And now the broken clouds above recalls to me this morning's fond parting. Oops!

He has stepped in a puddle.

Befuddled and tipsy he walks a crooked line, loses his way, but finally gets home.

Ukyo belches and then looks at the disguised Tamanoi.

UKYO: Ah, how fine to be master over another. Just as I commanded him, there he sits, completely unhappy.

Look, Tarokaja I have come back.
Did the old hag come to look for me?

The disguised Tamanoi shakes her hea· to indicate that, no, this did not occur.

What? She did not come?
Then that is just fine, but you must be tired.

Again Tamanoi shakes her head.

You are not? Well, that is just fine, too.

They say that when one's heart is filled with love, it shows all over the outside of a person. And I am so happy tonight that I am afraid the old shrew will find out about it, and that would be terrible.

But I have no other way than to tell you about this wonderful love affair tonight so just listen, will you?

Tamanoi nods: she will.

Then you will listen to my story? Oh, good fellow, good fellow. But first I want you to take off that coverlet . . .

But then, thinking about it, I see you must be a bit embarrassed at what I have to say so you just keep it on and stay as you are.

Tamanori nods that this is just what she will do.

Then you will listen? I am very happy.
Well . . .

First I went up and knocked on the double doors of her bedroom.
Knock-knock, I went. Knock-knock.

CHORUS: Then, with the voice of a nightingale coming from the mouth of the valley, she bade me welcome and quickly pushed open the doors. She raised the bamboo screens and the fair wind spread her fragrance. Then she took me into the inner room, the inner room of her heart, and poured out for me the paradise of her love.

Tamanoi angrily stamps her foot.

UKYO: You are supposed to be listening!

Anyway, Hanago continued:

CHORUS: You did not answer the letter I sent you and you have not come to see me and so I thought that you had either torn up and thrown away the letter or else had forgotten about me, and I have been drowned in tears.

At this I attempted to embrace her but she pushed me aside.

Yearning for you, my love, I came,
My heart inflamed with desire,
But are you crying to punish me,
Or did you really dislike me?
After all, I do love you,
And have come to see you again,
Even knowing that nothing will come of our love.

In this clever manner I led her on and very quickly she became smiling and compliant.

UKYO: And then she took me into the inner room and put this robe upon me.

Tamanoi stamps again.

Will you listen?

Then we had food and saké, and we had many, many things to talk about, and then we danced and sang . . .

CHORUS: Oh, we had a wonderful time together, and before we were able to end our playful lovers' quarrel, the voice of the bird could be heard. And, saying that I must take my leave, I got up but she pulled me by the sleeve and stopped me, and then . . .

Oh, no. I cannot stay, I cannot.

The old hag would be furious . . .

UKYO: And she nags so!

CHORUS: Well, she says, if you are so eager to return to your dearest wife, I should like to see her once myself.

What, you want to see that vixen's face?

Well, she is quite a sight, quite a sight.

Just let me describe her to you.

She has a most peculiar face,
A flat pug-nose,
And glaring eyes,
A face as black as charcoal
And altogether she looks like those singular monkeys that live in the mountains.

UKYO: And that is the end of my story. But be very careful that the old hag does not discover any of this: Do not forget.

Well, you may take off the coverlet now.

Tamanoi shakes her head, no.

UKYO: You do not want to? But, look, you cannot wear it forever just because you do not want now to take it off.

All right, then. I will take it off for you.

CHORUS: He takes it off and . . . woe is he!
There beneath is not Tarokaja, but . . .

TAMANOI: Ah-hah, you wretch!
So you think you fooled me!

UKYO: No, no. I just went to Tsukushi.

TAMANOI: And how could you go to Tsukushi, in the southern islands, in just one night? Tell me or I will tear you apart.

UKYO: No, no. I went to the Temple of Zenko in Shinano.

TAMANOI: That is another lie! Oh, but I am angry. I am angry!
And is no one around to catch hold of him? Oh, I am furious!

UKYO: Please, please forgive me.

CHORUS: The poor man babbles explanations, and begging pardon all the while he runs away.

Tamanoi begins chasing Ukyo about the stage and finally down the hanamichi.

But I will not let you get away, she cries, aflame with anger! And stamping her feet, she races and chases him out of the house.

CURTAIN

TAKATSUKI

WRITTEN BY HISAMATSU ISSEI IN IMITATION OF THE KYOGEN AND FIRST PERFORMED IN 1933.

THIS MODERN DANCE-PLAY WAS PATTERNED AFTER THE FARCIAL INTERLUDES WHICH RELIEVE THE SOLEMNITY OF THE NOH DRAMA. A GRAND LADY AND HER TWO SERVANTS ARE OUT VIEWING THE CHERRY-BLOSSOMS. WISHING TO ENJOY A CUP OF SAKÉ, THE LADY CALLS FOR A *TAKATSUKI*, THE PEDESTAL UPON WHICH THE CUP IS PLACED. FINDING THAT IT HAS BEEN FORGOTTEN, SHE SENDS ONE OF HER SERVANTS AFTER IT. THIS PARTICULAR SERVANT HAS NO IDEA WHAT A *TAKATSUKI* IS BUT HE PASSES A WOODEN-CLOG PEDDLER CRYING HIS WARES AND MISTAKES THE CLOGS (*TAKAASHI*) FOR THE PEDESTALS. OVERJOYED AT HAVING FINALLY, FOUND WHAT HE THINKS HIS MISTRESS WANTS, HE AND THE CLOG-DEALER DRINK UP THE SAKÉ. WHEN THE LADY FINALLY LOCATES THE MISSING SERVANT, SHE FINDS HIM COMPLETELY DRUNK.

CAST

THE GRAND LADY
TARO, *The Servant*
JIRO, *Another Servant*
THE CLOG PEDDLER
CHANTERS AND MUSICIANS

TAKATSUKI

The single scene of the play is the traditional Kabuki version of the Noh stage.

CHORUS: Today is a lovely day in the environs of Saga
And the cherry-blossoms hide the mountains,
Lose them in the mist of spring.
Viewing them come a lady and her servants.

The lady and her servants appear.

LADY: Oh, they are in full bloom.

JIRO: Yes, so they are. They have all come out.

LADY: The mountain, the fields, the banks and the roads . . .

JIRO: . . . look as though made of rose-colored mist.

LADY: And the fragrance of the blossoms quite tempt the nose.

TARO: It is the smell of the saké which tempts this nose.

LADY: Well, then, let us have a cup of saké.

Here, here, Taro. Bring the cups.

TARO: Yes.

LADY: Now, now. What do you mean by putting the cup on the ground like that? Bring the *takatsuki.*

TARO: Yes.

LADY: Well, why are you wandering about like that? I said to bring the *takatsuki.* Hurry now, bring the *takatsuki.*

Taro has never heard of a takatsuki *and does not know that this is the small stand upon which the saké is properly served. He does, however, remember a place-name which he thinks might help.*

TARO: *Takatsuki* . . . Oh, yes. Those famous *takatsu* dumplings of Mishima Oshu. My lady, then, would prefer dumplings to blossoms?

JIRO: No, no. You are wrong. A *takatsuki* is something you put the saké cup on. You hold it high, and respectfully offer the cup from it. It has little feet . . . it is a stand.

LADY: Well, if we do not have a *takatsuki,* then you will have to go around town until you can find one.

TARO: Yes.

LADY: You understand now?

And during that time I shall go to the temple and pray.

You go and hunt for one now—and hurry.

Well, let us go.

CHORUS: In the green grass
The shimmering of the dew
And all the thrown-away rice-ball wrappings
Make one truly think of spring.

The Lady and Jiro retire.

TARO: Now I wonder what kind of thing it was she was asking for. I have a good idea!

I will call out.

I want to buy a *takatsuki.*

The clog-peddler comes by, crying his wares.

PEDDLER: *Takaashi* for sale.

The main point of the play lies, of course, upon the possibilities of confusion between the word for saké-cup-pedestal (TAKATSUKI) and the word for wooden clog (TAKAASHI). These clogs are held onto the feet by thongs which pass between the big toe and the one next to it. Since they are used for walking outdoors, they are not flat on the bottom. Rather they have two 'teeth' or short legs which support the wearer. It is this kind of clog which the peddler is attempting to sell.

I am having a difficult time selling these. I was told to go and try to sell them to people viewing the blossoms. It rains now and again and the people need them to get over the puddles. And that is why I am trying to sell them here.

TARO: I want to buy a *takatsuki.*

PEDDLER: *Takaashi* for sale.

This is repeated until Taro says:

TARO: What was it you said just then?

PEDDLER: What was it that you said?

TARO: Well, I said that I wanted to buy a *takatsuki.*

PEDDLER: And I said that I was selling *takaashi.*

TARO: By *takaashi* do you perhaps mean the *takatsuki* upon which you place the saké cup?

PEDDLER: Oh, yes, yes. Anything you say.

TARO: Oh, then I am most happy.

My lady told me to buy a *takatsuki* and bring it to her.

PEDDLER: Then you are very fortunate, for I am that very *takatsuki* peddler.

TARO: Then the *takatsuki* is that thing you put the saké cup on and respectfully offer the cup off of?

PEDDLER: Yes, yes. You slide your feet, slowly . . . slowly . . . very respectable.

The peddler begins undoing his bundle.

TARO: But does a *takatsuki* have so many teeth?

PEDDLER: You need a pair for saké serving. You need one to place before the lord and one to put before his guest.

TARO: Well, what are these bands at the top for?

PEDDLER: Those are thongs.

TARO: And what are thongs?

The passage here depends upon a pun on the word O *which can mean either thong or the tail of an animal. The peddler, delighted to be selling, is saying, anything that comes into his head.*

PEDDLER: By that I mean . . . well, the cat's tail. You know, the cow's tail. Anyway, when you go on an excursion you hold it by this band.

TARO: You hold it by this band? But are *takatsuki* as high as this?

PEDDLER: Oh, yes, it is raised off the ground.

He continues and his next statement points out that an element of the word takatsuki *means high.*

And that is why they are called *taka-tsuki.*

TARO: Oh, I see. They raise things off the ground and that is why they are called *takatsuki.*

PEDDLER: So, you put the cup on it.

TARO: You put the cup on it.

The peddler illustrates.

PEDDLER: Well, since the cup is here, let us put some saké into it.

TARO: Yes, let us do that.

He takes the gourd which contains the saké and pours the cup full.

They continue to drink and as they do so, getting more and more drunk, they play poem-games.

PEDDLER: If your guest is a cultured man, he can compose a song and write it on the long poem-paper, but in order to hang it on the branch of the tree he will need something high to stand on.

TARO: That is true.

PEDDLER: So you put one of these on top of the other and then you step on both and then you can tie it to the branch.

Taro tries to make up a poem.

TARO: When you tie the love poem to the lovely cherry . . .

The peddler completes the verse to his own satisfaction.

PEDDLER: Then you spur the horse onward,
You ride under the tree,
And the beautiful blossoms
Fall to the ground.

TARO: Oh, good. That was very good.

PEDDLER: That storm coming up . . .

The chorus, taking this as a cue, begins a song in the popular style.

CHORUS: The cherry-blossoms,
They blossom for three days
But I do not get out to see them.
Then on the one time that I do.
I find them all covered with mud.

The peddler dances.

Oh, the lazy spring
And the good feeling of being drunk,
And although you look up at the pink branches,

You cannot reach them.
But you can wait
And then catch them in the palm of your hand,
And then throw them about,
This way,
And that.
And then you slowly fall asleep
In Higashiyama.

After this reference to the famed cherry-viewing mountain near Kyoto, the peddler notices that Taro has fallen asleep.

PEDDLER: Look at you!
Fallen flat and fast asleep.

He picks up the gourd.

But I am lucky.
There is still some left.

During the party, amid the moon and flowers,
The only thing I love is . . . this.

He indicates the saké-gourd, then begins laughing so hard that he wakes up Jiro, who at once begins laughing too, then falls asleep again.

PEDDLER: And when they view the cherry-blossoms
Even the court folk
Forget about their fine clothes
And get drunk
And sing and dance
And enjoy the saké much more than they do the flowers.

The peddler retires and the lady returns with the other servant. They call for Taro and finally find him.

JIRO: Taro! Here, here, my lady. He has fallen asleep. I will awaken him. Taro, Taro! Wake up.

He finally awakens, belches, and says:

TARO: No, no. I cannot drink any more.

LADY: This fellow has drunk all the saké.

JIRO: Oh . . . he has drunk all of madame's saké.

LADY: Instead of buying a *takatsuki* . . .

JIRO: . . . he has drunk all the saké in the gourd.

LADY: What a dreadful servant!

They strike him.

TARO: Oh, that hurts.

Ah, my lady, I have just returned.

LADY: Oh? And where is the *takatsuki?*

TARO: I brought them, I brought them.

LADY: What did you bring?

TARO: This is what I brought.

He puts the clogs before her.

JIRO: This is wrong. That is not a *takatsuki;* they are *takaashi.*

This discussion continues for some time, both the lady

and Jiro trying to make Taro comprehend. Finally the lady loses her temper and both she and Jiro begin beating him.

TARO: Oh, that hurts, that hurts.

Look, dear lady, they are really *takatsuki.* And this is the tail of a cat . . . or at least the tail of a fox.

This apparently reminds him of the peddler's song.

Oh, you spur your horse and you ride under the tree and all of the beautiful blossom fall to the ground.

Taro begins to dance.

JIRO: Listen, my lady. Taro has gotten completely drunk on all that saké.

LADY: So, instead of buying a *takatsuki,* he has gotten drunk on the saké.

And now look at him, dancing around like this.

Both the lady and Jiro turn upon the dancing Taro and say:

Be still!

CHORUS: While drinking,
While viewing the blossoms,
It is but natural,
To get drunk;
But natural,

TAKATSUKI

To come together,
And to ascend
To the mountain of spring.

CURTAIN

CHUSHINGURA

THE FORTY-SEVEN RONIN

WRITTEN BY TAKEDA IZUMO, MIYOSHI SHORAKU, AND NAMIKI SENRYU. FIRST STAGED AS A BUNRAKU PUPPET PLAY IN 1748, AND VERY SHORTLY AFTERWARDS ADAPTED FOR THE KABUKI STAGE.

THE FIRST OF THESE FOUR SCENES TAKEN FROM THE FIRST PART OF *CHUSHINGURA* OPENS DURING THE INAUGURATION OF THE GRAND HACHIMAN SHRINE AT KAMAKURA. THE DEPUTY OF THE SHOGUN IS BEING RECEIVED BY THE GOVERNOR OF KAMAKURA, KONO MORONAO, AND HIS TWO DEPUTIES, MOMONOI WAKASANOSUKE AND ENYA HANGAN. THE SHOGUN HAS SENT HIS YOUNGER BROTHER, TADAYOSHI, WHO ANNOUNCES THAT THE SHOGUN WISHES THE HELMET OF A NOBLE ENEMY, RECENTLY KILLED, TO BE LAID UPON THE NEW SHRINE. THERE IS THE PROBLEM OF IDENTIFYING THIS HELMET AMONG SO MANY UNTIL IT APPEARS THAT HANGAN'S WIFE WAS ONE OF THOSE IN CHARGE OF THE ARMOURY AND THAT SHE CAN IDENTIFY THE HELMET BY ITS ODOR, IT BEING THE HABIT OF NOBLES TO PERFUME THEIR HAIR BEFORE GOING INTO BATTLE SO THAT, IF KILLED, OR MUTILATED, THEIR HEADS WOULD BE RECOGNIZED AND GIVEN PROPER BURIAL.

LADY KAOYO, THE WIFE, IDENTIFIES THE PROPER HELMET BUT DURING THIS PROCEDURE IT BECOMES APPARENT THAT MORONAO IS MUCH attracted by her. He gives her a love letter and she, embarrassed, throws it away. Then he tells her plainly that her husband's career depends entirely upon herself. If she should yield, then Moronao will obey her in all things; if not, then her husband will suffer. The young Wakasanosuke interferes and the Lady Kaoyo escapes. Only the return of Tadayoshi and his suite saves Moronao from being killed by the young samurai then and there.

The second scene takes place within the palace, Moronao, furious at the virtue of the Lady Kaoyo, decides to bait her husband, Hangan. He insults him, knowing that the husband can do nothing in the palace, where fighting is a capital offense. But he goes too far and the gentle Hangan, unable to endure any more, wounds him on the forehead.

The third scene takes place a few days later in the mansion of Enya Hangan. The envoys from the Shogun have arrived with the order that Hangan, for causing a disturbance in the palace, should have his domains confiscated, and should commit *seppuku*—should disembowel himself. Just before dying Hangan asks for Yuranosuke but, upon being told that he is nowhere about, plunges the dagger into his abdomen.

YURANOSUKE COMES RUNNING UP THE *HANAMICHI* AND SUPPORTS HIS MASTER AS THE LATTER DRAWS THE DAGGER COMPLETELY ACROSS HIS STOMACH, DISEMBOWELING HIMSELF. HE TELLS YURANOSUKE THAT WITH THIS DAGGER HE MUST AVENGE THE DEATH OF HIS MASTER. THEN WITH A LAST EFFORT, HE DRAWS OUT THE DAGGER, CUTS HIS OWN JUGULAR VEIN AND FALLS FOR-WARD, DEAD.

THE FOURTH AND FINAL SCENE TAKES PLACE BEFORE THE GREAT GATE OF ENYA HANGAN'S MANSION. THE LOYAL SAMURAI OF HANGAN, NOW MASTERLESS AND HENCE CALLED RONIN, GATHER BEFORE THE GATE, CRYING FOR VENGE-ANCE. YURANOSUKE PERSUADES THEM THAT NOW IS NOT THE TIME BUT THAT THEY WILL HAVE THEIR REVENGE. AS THEY ARE SPEAKING THE BOLTS OF THE GREAT GATE ARE SHOT SHUT, THE SHOGUN'S MEN TAUNT THEM UPON THEIR MASTERLESS STATE, AND THE MEN UNWILLINGLY DISPERSE, EACH KNOWING IN HIS HEART THAT, IN TIME, THE DEATH OF THE MASTER WILL BE AVENGED.

YURANOSUKE, IN PERHAPS THE MOST FAMOUS SECTION OF THE PLAY, STANDS ALONE BEFORE THE GREAT GATE, LOOKS AT THE DAGGER, AND SILENTLY RENEWS HIS PLEDGE TO HANGAN. THEN, TURNING, HE GAZES AT THE MANSION WHICH WAS ONCE HIS HOME AND HIS FATHER'S BEFORE HIM. THUS END THESE SCENES FROM THE DAY-LONG

DRAMA, *CHUSHINGURA*, THE MOST POPULAR AND MOST BELOVED PLAY IN THE KABUKI REPERTOIRE. IN SUBSEQUENT SCENES, YURANOSUKE CARRIES OUT HIS REVENGE AND MORONAO IS KILLED. THEN, HE AND HIS MEN, THE RONIN, THEIR MISSION ACCOMPLISHED, COMMIT *SEPPUKU* AS DID THEIR LORD.

CAST

KONO MORONAO, *The Governor of Kamakura*
OBOSHI YURANOSUKE, *Samurai to Hangan*
ENYA HANGAN, *Daimyo to Moronao*
KAOYO, *His Wife*
MOMONOI WAKASANOSUKE, *Daimyo to Moronao*
ISHIDA UMANOJO, *The Shoguns's Envoy*
TADAYOSHI, *Brother to the Shogun*
SAGISAKA BANNAI, *Retainer to Moronao*
KAKOGAWA HONZO, *Councillor to Wakasanosuke*
YAKUSHIJI JIROZAEMON, *Confident of Moronao*
OBOSHI RIKIYA, *Yuranosuke's son*
ENYA'S SAMURAI
LORDS
SOLDIERS
ALSO, ATTENDANTS, SERVING GIRLS, MAIDS, ETC.
CHANTERS AND MUSICIANS

SCENE I

Before the Grand Hachiman Shrine of Kamakura during the inauguration ceremonies celebrating a recent victory and the ascent of a new Shogunate. The entire ceremonial procession is gathered upon the stage and the Gidayu-chanters begin the play.

CHORUS: Attention, attention . . .

True worth is not known until it is tried. Just as the excellence of a dish is not known until it is tasted . . .

Likewise, in times of peace the loyalty and bravery of a valiant warrior go unnoticed, like the invisible stars of daytime which shine only in the darkness of night. Such an example is herewith shown.

During the reign, of peace, Ashikaga Sahyoe no Kami, Lord Naoyoshi, younger brother of the Shogun, arrives in Kamakura as deputy to pay respects during the dedication of the Hachiman Shrine. In attendance, close at his side, is the arrogant Governor of Kamakura, Lord Moronao, Count of Musashi, who sits with overweening official pride, gazing condescendingly upon the officials assembled.

Delegated by the Steward to receive the guests of the dynasty are: Wakasanosuke Yasuchika, the younger brother of Momonoi, Lord of Harima; and Lord of Hakushiu, Enya Hangan Takasada, who has enclosed the grounds with a curtain. Both are solemnly executing their official duties and His Excellency Naoyoshi says:

NAOYOSHI: It is true that we have summoned you

forth, Lady Kaoyo, for the following purpose: In the past rebellion of the Benko era, Nitta Yoshisada was bestowed a helmet by the Emperor, a helmet which His Majesty himself had worn at the capital. Nitta was without doubt wearing that very helmet when he was defeated by our forces. But there is no one now who knows this helmet. If you recall his helmet, I bid you point it out.

CHORUS: Listening to this courteous request, Lady Kaoyo softly replies:

KAOYO: I am honored beyond merit by Your Excellency's command. Every morning and every evening in my care was His Majesty's helmet. Indeed, at the bestowal of both His Majesty's helmet and the famous incense *Ranjatai,* it was through my very hands that Nitta received them. In accepting the gifts, he said: "If there be a warrior on the battlefield who claims the head of a man wearing a helmet permeated with the famous fragrance of this incense, then let it be known that Nitta Yoshisada is dead."

His word I do not doubt.

CHORUS: Observing the lips of beautiful Lady Kaoyo, Moronao who has secret intentions, listens attentively.

Tadayoshi, too, listens carefully and commands his attendants:

TADAYOSHI: Men, have the Lady point out the helmet.

SOLDIERS: Yes, Your Excellency.

CHORUS: Complying with the wishes of His Excellency, promptly the lower attendants unlock the coffer and bring forth the helmets.

Without hesitation, Lady Kaoyo draws nearer.

The first to be examined is a helmet studded with the famous stars of Kamakura, and amongst the the many appears a five-tier helmet topped by a golden dragon. Even before Lady Kaoyo has identified the helmet, the fragrance of the famous incense permeates the air.

KAOYO: Your Excellency . . . , Yoshisada's helmet. That which I, Kaoyo, was accustomed to care for. This, without doubt . . .

CHORUS: . . . is this very one.

NAOYOSHI: Enya and Momonoi, store Yoshisada's helmet in the Treasury of this Hachiman Shrine.

Lady Kaoyo, you may retire.

KAOYO: My lord.

CHORUS: Dismissing the Lady Kaoyo and, followed by Enya and Momonoi, the Shogun's deputy and brother passes into the shrine.

Naoyoshi and his train leave the stage.

Lady Kaoyo, left thus, in embarrassment addresses Moronao.

KAOYO: My lord, my duty has been performed. I beg to take leave of your lordship.

CHORUS: As she is about to leave, she is detained.

MORONAO: One moment, Kaoyo. We are indebted for your service today. I have detained you because there is a matter which I wish to discuss with you.

KAOYO: Pray, what matter is this?

MORONAO: I am greatly devoted to poetry. Daily I have asked the poet Yoshida Kenko to assist me in a correspondence which is to be sent you. This letter then inquires whether you would wish to answer favorably or not. Do not hesitate to answer by word of mouth if you so desire.

CHORUS: The knotted love letter is passed from sleeve to sleeve. In contrast to his unpleasing features, the most elegant of titles are lettered on the envelope. Lady Kaoyo is surprised and silently throws it back. Fearing the eyes of others, Musashi hastily retrieves it . . .

Though spurned, I am satisfied, for the letter has been touched by her hands. But the letter is mine, and I cannot leave it here.

MORONAO: Until I receive a favorable answer, I shall persistently importune you and press my suit, until I succeed. Whether your husband, Enya Hangan, executes his duties successfully or not depends upon my will alone. Kaoyo, have you not given thought to this matter.

CHORUS: Hearing this, Kaoyo could answer with tears alone.

Wakasanosuke appears.

WAKASANOSUKE: Lady Kaoyo, have you not yet taken your leave? His Excellency has accorded you permission to retire. To remain here longer would be unfit. I urge you to withdraw immediately.

KAOYO: Your lordship, if you will permit, I shall take leave.

Kaoyo bows and retires.

CHORUS: Then Wakasanosuke has suspected something . . . so thought Moronao, but, to put an end to suspicions, he angrily exclaims:

MORONAO: Again you audaciously intrude! If Lady Kaoyo is to be permitted to withdraw, it is I who grant the withdrawal.

Lady Kaoyo has been desiring me to instruct her husband so that he may successfully discharge his duties. The situation warrants such courtesy. Even Enya, a lord of some standing, seeks my instructions, and what are you? . . . nothing but a no one of lowest rank!

Wakasanosuke becomes angry as Moronao continues.

Through whose secret favor did a nothing like yourself receive your rank? But a word from my mouth would suffice to lower you to a beggar from tomorrow. And you look upon yourself as a warrior, a samurai! You fool!

CHORUS: To requite the interference Moronao insolently unleashes his tongue. Wakasanosuke's anger mounts, but remembering that he was within the sacred precincts of the shrine and near the presence of His Excellency, he restrains himself . . . for one false word, one false move would mean the difference between life and death. Wakasanosuke, containing his anger, firmly grips the handle of his sword.

Then, unable to bear this shame . . . Wakasanosuke draws nearer, only to be interrupted by the escort's voices:

HERALD: His Excellency, Naoyoshi, is returning.

MORONAO: It's His Excellency's return. Hold!

Wakasanosuke restrains himself and the scene ends in a tableau, each in opposition to each other, striking the pose known as the nippari no mie.

SCENE II

The pine-room of the palace.

Wearing ceremonial dress, the nagabakama *or flowing*

trousers, the courtiers are gathered for the coming festivities, a continuation of the victory celebrations. In the background can be heard the music of the Noh musicians who have been assembled for the entertainment. Moronao and Hangan enter.

CHORUS: Enya Hangan, neither late nor early, proceeds along the corridor toward the presence of His Excellency. Incited by previous happenings Moronao angrily shouts:

MORONAO: You are late, you are late. What do you mean by this tardiness? You were instructed to be here at exactly four this morning. What has delayed you? You must observe court propriety.

HANGAN: It is my carelessness to have been late, my lord; still, I believed that there was yet ample time and thus the delay. I beg your lordship's pardon. First, sir, my servant has just delivered to me a letter box from my wife to be given to you.

MORONAO: What do you say? Something from your wife in that box. Truly, from your wife, addressed to me. Ah, I understand. You know that I have been a devoted of poetry for some time. Your wife had asked me to correct her verse; no doubt, it is an inquiry concerning this matter.

A further delay would not have mattered. There is still time to be spared. You may rest at ease.

Moronao takes the letter box.

I must say that your wife is an accomplished woman. I, too, have an irresistible passion for versemaking.

HANGAN: My lord, in your busy state of affairs, I deam it impolite for her to . . .

MORONAO: No, Hangan, it's a great diversion from my pressing duties. Let me see. I am sure it's an excellent verse.

Moronao opens the letter box and looks at the slip of paper on which is written a poem.

Even were it not so,
My simple bedrobe already lies heavily over me;
I cannot double the hem of my skirt
With the skirt which is not mine own.

Moronao rereads this poem, the meaning of which is hidden in a pun, the character, for skirt and for husband being similar.

This is taken from the New Anthology of Ancient and Modern Poems from the Chapter of Memoirs. No correction is necessary here.

He reads, then ponders.

CHORUS: After reflecting a moment, Moronao understands his suit to be rejected. Certain that Kaoyo had confided the matter to her husband, Enya, Moronao becomes angered but assumes an appearance of unconcern, then asks:

MORONAO: Enya, have you read this poem?

HANGAN: No, your honor, now is the first time that I am hearing it.

MORONAO: Is that so? I must say, Enya, your wife is a lady of virtue and talents. In this verse she so hastily penned, she shows herself accomplished in the art of calligraphy, and unmatched in diverse imagination. You may well be proud of her.

Your wife, Kaoyo, is renowned for her beauty and you hate to leave her side. You dote on your wife and ignore your duties.

CHORUS: Insinuating with an abusive and invective tongue, his suit having been rejected, Moronao works his vexation upon Enya. Unable to understand this conduct, Enya is deeply offended, but manages to control his indignation.

HANGAN: Your Lordship, Moronao, your words indicate that you are joking, or that you are intoxicated. It would seem you had perhaps been drinking.

MORONAO; No, I have not, Hangan. Tell me, when did you ever serve me a drink? And I, Lord of Musashi, whether intoxicated or not, have never failed to attend to my duties. Is it not you who are inebriated? Exchanging cups with your charming wife doubtless caused your tardiness. Naturally, I can well understand. If your wife is that precious, from tomorrow you need not attend office.

What was it they called men like you who stick to home? Ah, yes. In parables they are called carp enclosed in a well. Now, do not become angry. It is the truth. I'm telling you this for your future benefit. Listen well.

These little carp believe that there is no place better in heaven or earth than their miserable well, but a few feet across. When the well is cleaned these paltry fish happen to be caught in the well-bucket and through pity are thrown into the broad stream where they, unaccustomed to the vast waters, become wrought-up with joy and lose their way. They flounder here and flounder there until they finally knock their noses against a bridge post and crying . . . they die in agony.

These contemptible carp are just like you. You come from just such a well-like home and when you find yourself upon vast premises you helplessly meander; since you rarely have opportunity to inhabit such magnificent quarters as these, you are late for the appointed time. Near the pine-room you stand at unease. And when asked, Enya, why do not you attend your post of duty, bewildered you ask: 'Which way is my post, where can I find my post of duty?' And, so saying, you hurry here and scurry there, and at long last you knock your head against a pillar in the corridor and die crying . . . in agony.

And this carp . . .

How strange . . . I must say, Enya Hangan, you look more and more like a carp.

Enya becomes angry.

There, there, when you are furious you show a perfect likeness to the carp!

Through all the years I've lived, this is the first time I've seen a carp clothed in formal attire appearing in such quarters as these. Do you hear, Bannai? Enya Hangan has become a carp. He is the very image of that noble, knightly fish.

CHORUS: Thus he said whatever he pleased, whatever occurred to his mind, and Enya Hangan, no longer able to suppress his anger, says:

HANGAN: This Lord of Hakushiu, Enya Hangan Takasada, you have contemptably insulted. You must be out of your senses; I say, you have gone mad, Lord of Musashi!

MORONAO: Hold your tongue, Hangan. How dare you to accuse me, Moronao, the highest dignity in presence here, of being mad.

HANGAN: Then your insulting remarks have been responsible and you have spoken in earnest?

MORONAO: Of course, in earnest. And, that being so, what do you intend to do?

HANGAN: If you meant what you said in earnest...

MORONAO: And if I did, then what?

Hangan begins to unsheathe his sword.

MORONAO: You, sir, are within palace quarters!

He strikes Enya hard with his fan and Enya controls himself, Moronao smiles.

Remember, you are within the palace.

HANGAN: Yes.

MORONAO: If you unsheathe your sword more than three fingers' width within the palace, it means the complete ruin of your household. Are you aware of that? I think you are aware of that. Well, if you know it and still want to strike me, I will allow you to do so. Well, strike, go ahead and strike me. Strike, Hangan.

HANGAN: Your lordship, please wait. I beg forgiveness for my previous rashness. Please be of good heart and I beseech you to direct my duties.

Moronao haughtily turns aside. Unable to restrain his anger, Hangan again grips the sword hilt. Moronao is startled and looks at him.

MORONAO; What do you intend to do with those hands?

HANGAN: These hands . . .

MORONAO: Yes, your hands.

HANGAN: With these two hands I prostrate myself and humbly beg your forgiveness.

MORONAO: So you apologize. Very well, than I shall allow today's banquet preparations and all reception matters to be put in charge of . . .

HANGAN: Then you will place me in charge of . . .

MORONAO: No, I do not mean you. I mean Wakasanosuke.

HANGAN: What!

MORONAO: Of such matters a barbarian-warrior like yourself would be ignorant.

Moronao throws the poem at Hangan's feet. He begins to walk calmly away. Hangan, unable to contain himself, purposely steps on the flowing trousers.

HANGAN: Moronao, wait!

MORONAO: Here, here. Out of the way . . .

You will tear my robes. Out of the way.

Or do you still have some business with me?

HANGAN: Yes, and that business is . . .

MORONAO: That business is . . .

HANGAN: You scoundrel!

Hangan strikes Moronao. The music quickens. Voices are heard. Other lords come out. From behind a screen comes Honzo who holds Hangan from behind. Assisted by Bannai, Moronao escapes. Hangan throws his sword at Moronao.

SCENE III

A room in Hangan's mansion. It is decorated with the encircled hawk feather crest of the Hangan family. In the center sits Hangan in the white robes of immolation, on mats laid upside down and covered with white cloth. At each corner is a twig of the Chinese anise, branches of which are usually placed only as offerings before Buddhist altars. At one side are seated Ishido and Yakushiji, commissioners of the Shogun.

CHORUS: Submitting to his orders, Rikiya, son of Yuranosuke, brings forth before his lord Enya, the official suicidal sword, which he had previously prepared.

Rikiya brings the small sword on its unpainted wooden stand. He prostrates himself before his lord. Hangan quietly indicates that he should leave, but Rikiya is reluctant. Sharply, with his eyes, Enya commands him to leave. He is obliged to leave and slowly retires.

CHORUS: Calmly, Enya removes the shoulder-folds of his kimono and prepares himself.

He draws the wooden stand toward himself and takes up the short sword which he lifts respectfully to his forehead.

HANGAN: Rikiya!

RIKIYA: Yes, my lord.

HANGAN: Where is Yuranosuke?

RIKIYA: He has not yet arrived, your lordship.

HANGAN: Alas!

CHORUS: Drawing the wooden stand toward him and taking the sword in hand . . .

HANGAN: Rikiya, Rikiya.

RIKIYA: Yes, sir.

HANGAN: Where is Yuranosuke?

RIKIYA: I regret to say, he has not yet arrived.

HANGAN: Tell him that I greatly regretted not being able to see him once again in life.

Commissioners, I beg you to witness this suicide.

CHORUS: Holding the swords towards him, he pushes the blade into his left side and then draws it across. Pushing open the panel doors of the corridor Yuranosuke hurries in. No sooner has he seen the plight of his lord than he quickly prostrates himself.

ISHIDO: Are you his chief councillor, Oboshi Yuranosuke?

YURANOSUKE: I am, your honor.

ISHIDO: Dispense with formalities. You may come closer.

YURANOSUKE: Thank you, your honor.

CHORUS: Soon after, the retainers hurry in.

YURANOSUKE: I, Oboshi, Yuranosuke have just come.

HANGAN: Oh, is it you, Yuranosuke?

YURANOSUKE: Yes, my lord.

HANGAN: How I've waited for you!

YURANOSUKE: And how grateful I am that I am able to see my lord's face in life.

HANGAN: I, too, am happy.

No doubt, you have heard the circumstances . . .

YURANOSUKE: Yes, my lord.

HANGAN: I am deeply mortified.

YURANOSUKE: No more, my lord . . . and I, too, have nothing more to say. I only pray that my lord's death will be one befitting a warrior.

HANGAN: I am aware of that.

CHORUS: So saying he places both hands on the sword and widens the wound. Gasping for breath, he pauses:

HANGAN: Yuranosuke, Yuranosuke!

YURANOSUKE: Yes, my lord.

HANGAN: This sword I'm giving to you as a pledge. Do you understand . . . as a pledge.

YURANOSUKE: I understand your intentions.

CHORUS: With the point of his sword he cuts his throat and, throwing aside his bloodstained sword, he collapses . . . dead.

The retainers, sitting in a row, filled with horror and sorrow, close their eyes and beneath their breath they grind their teeth, silently expressing grief and rage.

YAKUSHIJI: Now that Hangan is dead and gone, leave the mansion.

ISHIDO: Yuranosuke, I fully understand your distress. If I can be of any service to you, do not hesitate to call upon me.

After bowing to the retainers he turns to go. Rikiya stands at one side, intending to show him to the door.

ISHIDO: Thank you, but do not trouble yourself.

CHORUS: Composed, he takes his departure. Yuranosuke comes forward, removes the sword from Hangan's hand and places it within his bosom. Enya's wife, though still young, has shorn her tresses, signifying her renouncement of this world.

One of the ladies-in-waiting places Kaoyo's tresses before Yuranosuke.

KAOYO: Yuranosuke, look at this; you understand the significance . . . .

CHORUS: Yuranosuke tries to console Kaoyo who gives way to grief.

The party leaves for the family burial temple of Hangan.

The stage revolves.

SCENE IV

Before the gate of Enya Hangan's mansion.

CHORUS: The young samurai, who have just escorted their lord's body to the temple, hasten back to the mansion. Headed by Rikiya, they rush in. From within the gate appear Yuranosuke and the elder retainers. Yuranosuke stops them, then glances at his son, Rikiya.

YURANOSUKE: Rikiya, is it you? What do you mean by this warlike rushing here? All of you, despite my pleas, will you not listen to me?

RETAINERS: But we have good reason to . . .

YURANOSUKE: I have no choice. I will kill myself here. Someone please assist me.

RETAINERS: What answer have we to give?

YURANOSUKE: Then will you listen to me?

ALL: We wish to obey, but . . .

YURANOSUKE: Then, please restrain yourselves.

From within the gate the voice of Yakushiji is heard.

YAKUSHIJI: Ha! Look, men! Look and laugh at the wretched and suddenly masterless samurai. Let us laugh!

The soldiers within the gates laugh.

RETAINERS: Such derision we cannot tolerate!

YURANOSUKE: Here, withdraw, withdraw!

The men leave the stage.

CHORUS: Then, gazing ... gazing at the blood-stained sword, tears of sorrow and of passion flood his eyes.

Yuranosuke gazes at the great gate. He takes the lantern and from its paper tears the family crest, putting it in his bosom. He turns again to the great gate which moves slowly backward from him—he is leaving forever.

CHORUS: The misery of Hangan's last words reach the depths of both his body and his soul.

It is at this very moment that within him rise the sentiments of an unfaltering loyalty that have made his name eternally reknowned.

In deep thought, Yuranosuke leaves the hanamichi.

CURTAIN

POSTSCRIPT

The visit of the Kabuki to America in the late spring of 1960 was a theatrical event of the greatest importance. Though the company—Shochiku's Nakamura Troup from the Kabuki-za—has been abroad, it had never been to the United States, had never performed before a New York audience, one of the world's most sophisticated, and certainly one of the most intolerant. The American backers feared that the Americans would not like what they saw; the Japanese feared that the foreigners would not understand. That the New York performances were almost completely sold out before they began calmed no fears and the dress rehearsal was a shambles: the *hanamichi*, built into the City Center Theater just the day before, was too short; the *mawari-butai* stuck; the big gift curtain was too big for the proscenium; the running curtain would not run; the actors were not yet used to the cuts in the plays; there was stage-hand trouble; the transistor radio translation-units would not work in certain parts of the house. Yet the performance, two hours later, was perfection itself. That first performance of *Kanjincho* has been called "one of the finest of this century," and it was said that "if these performances had been given at the Kabuki-za they would have made theatrical history." What had happened is what usually happens between dress rehearsal and first-night but further meaning was given in that two groups of people, neither of which understood the language of the other, were doing their best for each other. From opening night there was real rapport at City Center, initially that of good-will, but rapidly growing into something more. The Americans backstage and the Japanese onstage were engaged in something important, and even the most cynical stage-hand, even the most mistrustful minor actor, eventually realized this. It was a real collision of East and West.

The American audience was ready for the Kabuki. Every seat was sold and the troupe could easily have played another month. The reviews were almost entirely enthusiastic and, upon those occasions when they were not, respectful. And the same people kept coming again and again: Garbo was one, another was Anne Bancroft, another was Irene Worth. There were others too, not famous, but faces one would recognize in the intermissions or after the performances, someone one had seen there before. The audience was intelligent and completely receptive. After the first performance of *Dojoji* the applause thundered, as it never does at the Kabuki-za. Utaemon stood in front of the curtain almost bewildered, then he stepped forward, smiled, pleased, and took bow after bow.

Bowing was one of the things the actors had to

learn. Before the opening performance they all lined up before the running curtain and were taught the proper way. At first they thought it was not necessary, that no one would understand and that there would be no applause. But they took their bowing lessons and after the first performance of *Kanjincho* the ovation caught Shoroku by surprise. He stood on the *hanamichi*, astonished, as the applause rose higher and higher, filling the whole auditorium, while he stood, straight and small, bowing cordially, and completely amazed.

After the first performance of *Chushingura*, Kanzaburo said: "I have never played before an audience like this one. It really pays attention. It watches. It tries to understand everything. During the middle of the *seppuku* scene I usually look up. Tonight I got the most terrible shock. I looked up and there were two thousand eyes looking straight back at me. I couldn't see them but I could feel them. And the quiet in the theatre. I could hear myself breathe. Never in my life have I played before an audience like this."

Originally the actors were nervous about the performances, about the audience. Before the first, and only rehearsal of *Tsubosaka*, Utaemon smoked two cigarettes in a row, a rare occurrence, and then gave a brilliant performance. There were some displays of temperament but not many. Utaemon once lost his temper during the *Dojoji* rehearsal when the big bell failed to descend on time. Most of the time, however, the actors were more relaxed than they are in Japan, there was more camaraderie, the hierarchy was not insisted upon. Utaemon and Kanzaburo both came to a party given for the young actors and apparently enjoyed themselves. They soon came to enjoy the performance as well and each knew precisely which parts the audience liked best. These, more or less in order, were: the final scene of the four from *Chushingura*, Yuranosuke before the gate of Enya Hangan; the *seppuku* from the same play; all of *Kanjincho*, the ending in particular; the *oiran-dochu* from *Kagotsurube*; all of *Migawari Zazen*, particularly the ending; and the final dance from *Takatsuki*. The only play that was not cared for (though Utaemon was always singled out for praise) was *Tsubosaka*, included by Shochiku only because it had been a success when the Kabuki toured Russia in 1928. Shochiku apparently thought that what the Russians had presumably liked thirty years ago the Americans would now.

Naturally, all the plays were cut: *Kanjincho* had the Buddhist liturgy removed; there were only four scenes from *Chushingura;* the slower middle sections of *Dojoji* were missing; parts of *Tsubosaka* were gone, though both *Migawari Zazen* and *Takatsuki* were more or less entire; and only five scenes, later four, from *Kagotsurube* were given. Of all these plays it was the last which gave the most trouble. The processions of the courtesans had great success, but the rest of the play sags and the final scene where Jiro kills Yatsuhashi never had the force it sometimes does in context of the entire play. The actors realized this and some attempt was made to salvage the finale. The Kabuki being, above all else, an actors' theater, the changes were sometimes arbitrary, often sweeping, and always sudden. Originally, and in the standard Kabuki-za version, Jiro kills Yatsuhashi with his sword, then kills the serving-girl with the lamp, takes a stance and looks at the sword, saying: "Ah, Kagotsurube, you cut well." This was the way it was done opening night. At the second performance the actors changed it: the serving-girl no longer came on and Jiro merely looked at his sword. Two nights later there was a new version: Jiro, after killing the courtesan, knelt and made as though to kill himself as the curtain was drawn. This lasted only two nights. After that the original was used with the difference that the servant-girl comes on chattering about having brought a light. Jiro, transfixed by the sight of the dead Yatsuhashi, merely motions the girl to be quiet. Unfortunately, he has a sword in one hand when he does so—thus, she too dies. Likewise the lines were changed. Almost every night the banquet scene was done differently, Kanzaburo reinstating lines or taking out, which was particularly harrowing for the interpreters who were working from the synchronized text and who suddenly found themselves with too much material or, worse, not enough.

The idea of transistor-radio translations came originally from the system in use at the United Nations, a simultaneous translation with the difference that, for the Kabuki, both languages would be so synchronized that common words, names and so on, would appear simultaneously in both the actors' and the translators' delivery. For this reason a pre-recorded or taped translation was impossible. Every stage performance is different from every other and this is particularly true of the Kabuki. Sometimes the tempo would be fast, sometimes slow, and this varied from performance to performance. The problem was that a live performance in English had to synchronize and that the cadences of the two languages had to be rendered identical. Just as important was the question of tone since colloquial translations were out of the question—the Japanese, even if one understood not a word, was obviously a formal language. The finished translations were stylistically quite interesting. The Kyogen plays, *Migawari Zazen* and even the 1937 *Takatsuki*, were done very lightly, somewhat in the manner of a Ben Jonson masque—simple language, with no archaic references, but one in which slight formalities underlined the humor. *Dojoji*, impossible to translate literally, with its obscure references, its puns, its pillow-words, taken straight from the Noh, was given as narrative. *Tsu-*

bosaka, so much a 19th Century play, was done in the style of Belasco, a style which presumes real snow seeping under a real door during a real snow-storm —it was also artificially inflated in the slightly hysterical manner of 19th Century American stage diction. *Chushingura* came out Shakespearian, but something from the mannerist period, a kind of less cruel *Measure for Measure.* The most interesting stylistically was *Kagotsurube.* Like most *sewamono,* the play itself resembles Restoration drama, so it was done in the style of minor Dryden, of Otway. The big set pieces (for example, that beginning: "Courte-san, you are too unkind!") were treated as though they were arias—which in a way they are.

Originally the actors did not like the idea of the simultaneous translations. Kanzaburo objected: "It will get in our way, it will obscure our big moments." To which he was answered: "If the translation is not there then the audience will not know a big moment when it sees one." After *Chushingura,* however, Kanzaburo was impressed. "What did you say to keep them so quiet?" he asked. "Nothing at all," was the answer: "Merely what you yourself said." Kanzaburo smiled: "Well, together we really captured them then." Shochiku, on the other hand, liked the idea of the transistors and insisted that they be used continually, that not a moment of silence be allowed to intervene. The Japanese backers would not believe, until it was demonstrated to them, that the simple dialogue was quite enough. They had originally wanted commentary and explication as well, covering the "difficult" parts. They would not believe that there were no difficult parts—their ideal was presumably something like those Japanese announcers who "explain" throughout the length of, say, a Mozart opera on the radio. Their suggestions were successfully resisted, however, and one of the results was that the audience was allowed to appreciate what was happening. The appreciation may have been superficial but it was probably not much more superficial than that of the usual audience at the Kabuki-za.

The appreciation was in some ways extreme. It showed itself in small ways: in the silence, in the attention, in the sale of libretti after the performance, and in the actions of certain members of the audience. For example, the day that Garbo went backstage. She insisted. The reason for going was to see Utaemon. Faubian Bowers took her back, knocked on Utaemon's dressing-room door and asked if it were all right if Garbo came in. "Who?" asked Utaemon, incredulous. Then: "No, it is not. I am old and not pretty at all. It is much better if she sees me all made up. Besides, I am all sweaty." This was translated to Garbo who indicated her enthusiasm, her simple regard for the actor with: "But, I want to see his sweat." She did not get in but, once made up, Utaemon came out and they talked. Then he took his place for the opening of *Chushingura*.

Just before the curtain was slid aside, Garbo stepped onto the stage and touched Utaemon on the shoulder. Startled, he turned around and she waved. He waved back, smiling, the *hyoshigi* sounded, Garbo ran from sight, and the curtain opened. Afterwards she is said to have said: "This is the most wonderful theatrical experience I have ever had."

Utaemon's success was complete, and this despite some fears as to how the *onnagata* would be received in America. Shochiku was particularly worried that the audience would laugh or would in some other way misunderstand but nothing of the sort occured. The audience quite accepted the convention of the *onnagata*. Another thing which threatened trouble was the fact that the Anti-Security Pact riots were occuring in Tokyo just as the Kabuki was opening in New York. This too, however, did not reflect upon the actors and the one comment one heard from members of the audience was: "How embarrasing it must be for the actors to be in America just as this is occuring in Japan." Likewise, there had been some fears that some remnants of anti-Japanese feeling would be visible—though World War II was fifteen years in the past. There was, however, very little of this. Among the hundreds who came backstage or to the stage-door afterward there were just two who mentioned the war. Likewise, almost no one left during the performances themselves, at the most two or three people, and their reasons could well be that, whatever they had expected, Kabuki was not it.

The actors soon became used to their audience just as they soon became used to life in America. Originally they had been a bit nervous, particularly about New York. They all arrived in Western suits, tended to stay in their hotel room or to go out in large groups. As the stay continued, however, they found their way about the city, and grew to like the fact that in kimono people turned and looked at them. The main actors, Utaemon, Kanzaburo, and Shoroku, as well as the late Tokizo, were taken from one party to the other and made a fuss over. The minor actors, however, were left more or less to themselves. Finally it was realized that none of them was eating properly and that one of the reasons was that they were afraid of the restaurants, first because they could not read the menus, and second because the American custom of tipping terrified them. Eventually they were taken to a large cafeteria near their hotel. There they could see what they wanted and get it by pointing, and since it was self-service there was no question of the tip. At least twice a day the cafeteria was enlivened by almost the entire Kabuki troupe in full kimono descending for a meal. The main actors were almost always taken out for lunch and supper but each found something they liked to do during their free time. Utaemon soon discovered the shops on Fifth and Madison Avenues and during one of his many shopping tours acquired an enormous koala bear, stuffed, which he often carried around with him. Kanzaburo was found of the theater. *The Miracle Worker* was playing in New York at the time and his admiration was Anne Bancroft was extreme—he once spend almost fifteen minutes on television talking about her. Also, it was quite mutual because Miss Bancroft was always found at the Kabuki. Shoroku liked baseball and, whenever he could, went off to Brooklyn or the Bronx to catch a game. Occasionally the actors were taken together to some particular function. One afternoon they were invited to the Actors' Studio to watch a rehearsal. They sat there, polite in full kimono, mystified by young actors all of whom looked and acted like Marlon Brando or Susan Strasberg telling each other;

"You got to feel it. It's got to be in the guts."

"What, please," asked Kanzaburo, "is the guts?"

"You know . . . you got to . . . it's got to project."

"Oh."

The Kabuki actors sat in a row looking at the "method" for an hour and a half and then a young director came up to talk Stanislavski with Shoroku, who speaks no English, or very little.

Shoroku smiled, had an inspiration and said: "Chekhov."

Others gathered round. One said: "Shaw!" to which Shoroku said: "Ibsen."

There was some disappointment when someone said, "Beckett!" and Shoroku said nothing. But everyone smiled again when a voice in back called "Giraudoux," and Shoroku said: "Cocteau."

POSTSCRIPT

"Boy," said one of the Actors' Studio people, "they really know their theater."

The Kabuki broke all attendance records at New York's City Center. It was financially successful in that—despite the great cost of sending the entire troupe, with musicians, technicians, scenery and costumes—it lost no money, and it gave pleasure to thousands. No one who ever saw this series of performances will ever forget them, this culmination of East and West working together. One continues to remember Utaemon, bowing, surprised and pleased; to remember Kanzaburo rushing into the wings to congratulate the American production manager after opening night; to remember those long waits between afternoon and evening performances when the stagehands at City Center learned *go* from the Japanese technicians, when minor actors took long conversation-filled walks with the grips and the electricians; when Shoroku, rather than take his nap, played cards backstage, or just sat smiling at New York.

These notes are reprinted with the permission of *Orient / West, Today's Japan,* the *New York Times, The Japan Times,* and *Geijutsu Shincho.*

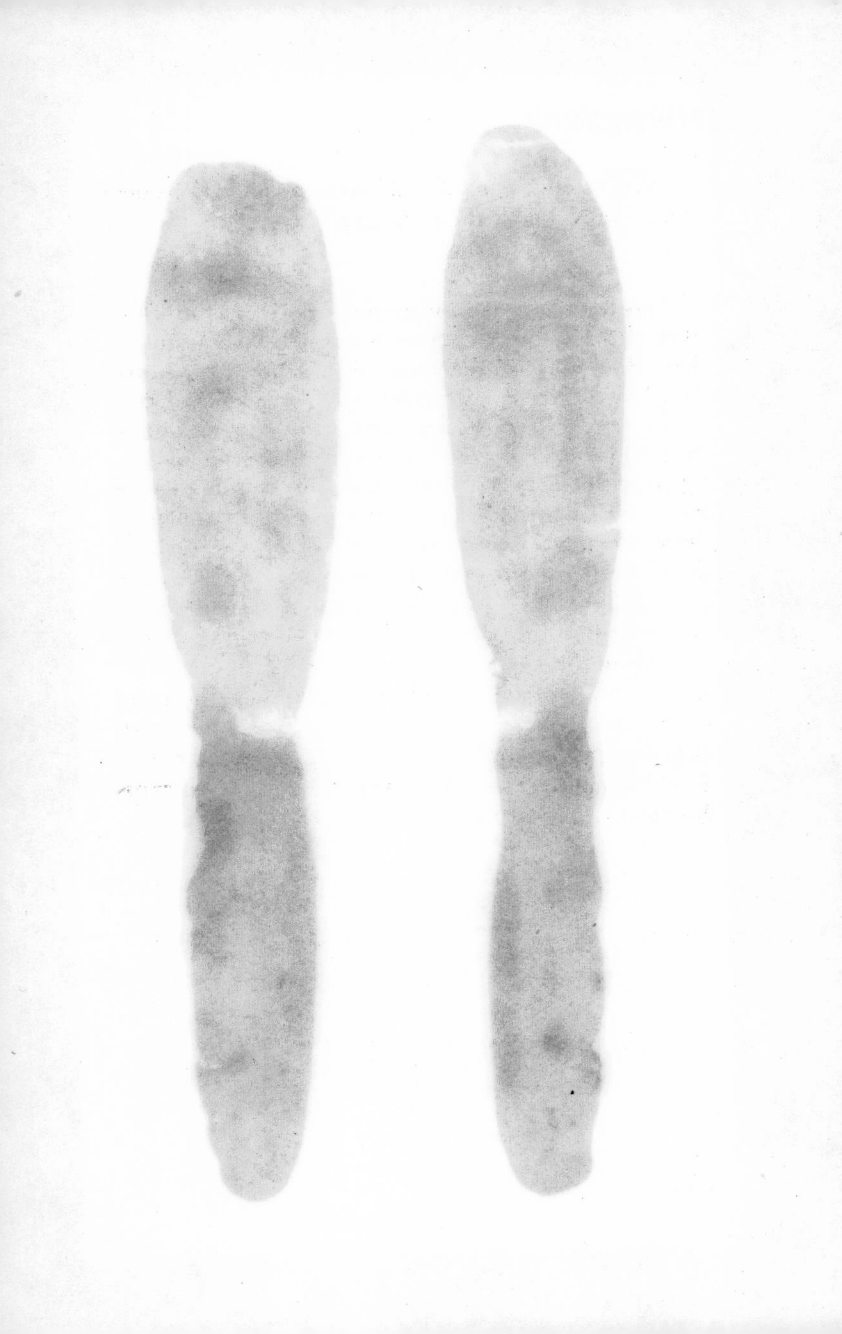

DATE DUE
